# THE

# MOST DIRECT MEANS

# TO

# ETERNAL BLISS

Volume One

Michael Langford

Sixth Edition July 2008

ISBN-13: 978-0-9797267-8-1

ISBN-10: 0-9797267-8-6

Published by

The Freedom Religion Press

www.thefreedomreligionpress.com

Previously published under the titles

The Most Direct and Rapid Means to Eternal Bliss

The Most Rapid and Direct Means to Eternal Bliss

The Imposter

# CONTENTS

# INTRODUCTION

## AND HOW TO READ THIS BOOK

1.    For thousands of years humans have been stuck in the same pool of inward unsolved problems.

2.    Thousands of years ago humans had the problems of suffering, sorrow, anger, fear, violence, conning, cheating, lying, death, etc.

3.    Today humans have the problems of suffering, sorrow, anger, fear, violence, conning, cheating, lying, death, etc.

4.    All of those problems have a single cause.

5.    In this book the cause of the lack of progress and the solution that actually works is revealed.

6.    There is a secret, a missing link, a vicious circle, that is keeping humans stuck in the same pool of unsolved problems.

7.    That secret, that missing link, that vicious circle is revealed in this book.

8.    How to break free of that ancient human trap is also revealed in this book.

9.    The solutions taught in the past have failed.

10.    Not even one in a million humans has been freed from all suffering and been established in absolutely perfect infinite-eternal-awareness-love-bliss by the solutions that have been taught in the past.

11.    It is possible to be free of all sorrow and suffering and to experience absolutely perfect infinite eternal joy here and now in this lifetime.

12.    It is possible for all humans, not just a few humans.

13.    There is a rapid means to infinite bliss.

14.    That rapid means is taught in this book.

15.    The strategies the ego uses to avoid liberation and how to end those strategies are also revealed in this book.

16.    Whatever spiritual path you are on, this book will be a great help.

17.    The problem of the ego distorting, distracting and keeping the attention directed outward is a problem shared by all humans, whatever path they are on.

18.    The ego's tricks have seldom been looked at in spiritual literature.

19.    The ego's tricks are revealed in this book.

20.    How to put an end to the ego's tricks is also taught in this book, making this book a unique and immensely valuable contribution.

21.    This book is a great help to all humans, including those who are not on a spiritual path, because the most direct and rapid means to end suffering and sorrow and to live in awareness-love-bliss, is of benefit to all.

# HOW TO READ THIS BOOK

22.   When humans are taught to read in school, they are taught to accumulate information and store it in memory in order to be able to pass a test.

23.   If this same approach to reading is used when reading an authentic spiritual teaching, the human will miss what is being conveyed.

24.   A completely different approach to reading is needed for spiritual reading.

25.   The purpose of an authentic spiritual teaching is to awaken an experience.

26.   The purpose of an authentic spiritual teaching is to awaken insight.

27.   To awaken insight, read very slowly.

28.   Stay with one sentence for a very long time before proceeding to the next sentence.

29.   Do not let the ego, which has misled humans for as long as there have been humans, prevent you from recognizing the unique value of what is being revealed in this book.

30.   This book contains only that which is most essential.

31.   This book is filled with hundreds of unique precious gems.

32.   Do not allow the ego's arguments to prevent you from seeing what is being revealed in this book.

33.   Do not allow the ego to distort what is being revealed in this book.

34.   Do not allow the ego to add to what is being conveyed in this book, for that too is a method the ego uses to distort.

35.   This book is a step-by-step instruction manual.

36.   This book is not for the purpose of intellectual entertainment.

37.   For human consciousness to be transformed, something new must be introduced.

38.   This book introduces something new into human consciousness.

39.   Infinite Love-Bliss is available in this lifetime.

40.   This book is something quite unique in the history of spirituality.

41.   There is something new under the sun.

42.   This book is a quantum leap out of the limited, ego-contaminated, spiritual teachings of the past.

43.   The reason the spiritual teachings of the past have failed to expose the tricks of the ego is because the spiritual teachings of the past serve the ego.

44.   What is surprising is the very large number of people who have already recognized, even at this very early date, the great value of this book, and more importantly, what this book is pointing towards.

# CHAPTER ONE

## THE IMPOSTER

1.   These are the definitions of the words *ego, Self* and *thought* that will be used in this book:

2.   *THOUGHT:*   Thoughts are the words of your language in your mind.

3.   If your native language is English and you write in English and speak English, those same English words in your mind are thoughts.

4.   Some people may speak, write and think in more than one language.

5.   *EGO:* ego is the thought I.

6.   The ego is the "I thought."

7.   "I am happy." "I am sad." "I did this." "I did that."   There are so many sentences in thought that contain the word "I." That thought "I" in each of those sentences is the ego.

8.   The ego is the idea of a separate, individual identity.

9.   The ego identifies with the body and with thought and calls the body and thought "I."

10.   The ego is thought.

11.   The ego is thinking.

12.  *SELF:* the Self is infinite-eternal-awareness-love-bliss.  Those are five words pointing towards one-awareness.  Awareness-love-bliss are not three, they are one.

13.  The Self is the background of awareness.

14.  Because almost all humans are in the habit of looking outward towards thoughts, the body, the world, people, places, things, etc., it appears as though the background of awareness (the Self) wakes up in the morning and goes to sleep at night.

15.  If you turn your attention towards the background of awareness, eventually you will discover: the background of awareness is continuous.

16.  Because almost all humans are in the habit of looking outward towards thoughts, the body, the world, people, places, things, etc., it appears as though the background of awareness is limited.

17.  If you turn your attention towards the awareness that wakes up in the morning, instead of towards people, places, things, thoughts, etc., eventually you will discover that awareness is infinite-eternal-awareness-love-bliss.

18.  The background of awareness that wakes up in the morning is there during all the waking hours until one goes to sleep at night.

19.  Thoughts come and go, but the background of awareness that is aware of the thoughts is there during all the waking hours and does not come and go.

20.  The background of awareness is the true Self.

21.   Before you learned the language you now think in, the background of awareness was there.

22.   Then you learned the word "I" in your language.

23.   Your body was given a name and when people saw that body they said "There goes John" (or Mike, or Jane, or Julie, or Kumar, or Radha) or whatever name they gave your body.

24.   Thus the idea arose "I am John, I am this body."

25.   You existed as the background of awareness before that I-thought arose.

26.   The thought calling its "self" "I" is an imposter "self."

27.   The background of awareness is the true Self.

28.   The fact that you existed before you learned the language that became your thoughts helps to reveal the difference between your true Self and the imposter.

29.   Because you existed as the background of awareness before you learned the language that produced the thoughts you now think in, you can easily see that the thought "I" is an imposter.

30.   All thoughts are opposed to your real nature.

31.   You know that thoughts are not part of your true nature because you had to learn them.

32.   That is why you cannot speak, write and think fluently in two hundred different languages: because you have not acquired those languages.

33.   You can observe that same process in an infant.

34.   You can see that an infant is aware before it learns any language.

35.   You can observe the child growing older and learning a language.

36.   You can observe when the child learns the word "I" and when the child begins to say the word "I."

37.   Being able to see how the imposter arose in you and how the imposter arises in every human infant and child is a very important tool.

38.   The reason it is a very important tool is: you do not have to rely upon someone else to tell you that the ego is an acquired imposter.

39.   You can observe this for yourself.

40.   Thought is something foreign, alien to the true Self.

41.   Thought pretends to be the Self.

42.   Thought is not the Self.

43.   Thought is an imposter.

44.   Thought believes thought is a real entity and thought believes thought is a real self.

45.   Thought is not a real entity and thought is not a self.

46.   Living from thought instead of living from Awareness is the cause of all human suffering.

47.   The imposter (thought – ego) is the cause of all human problems, sorrow and suffering.

48.   The background of awareness is the true Self.

49.   The awareness, that appears to wake up in the morning, is the true Self.

50.   The awareness that is looking through your eyes now is the true Self.

51.   As an example for clarification, you could view thinking and memory as something like a computer program.

52.   Within that computer program is a virus.

53.   The virus is called the "I thought."

54.   The virus controls the program.  The "I thought" controls all thinking.

55.   The virus pretends to be your self.   The "I thought" pretends to be your self.

56.   The virus creates tremendous sorrow and suffering.  The "I thought" creates tremendous sorrow and suffering.

57.   None of the sorrow or suffering is needed.

58.   What is needed is to delete the virus that pretends to be your self.  What is needed is to delete the imposter self.

59.    When one attempts to delete the virus, the virus sends out many thoughts claiming that deleting the virus is not a good idea.

60.    The virus has many strategies to preserve the illusion that it is real and to continue the delusion that it is the real self.

61.    In humans the program that came from the outside and took control of their awareness is called thought, language, and thinking.

62.    In humans the virus is called the ego or the "I thought."

63.    The "I thought" (ego) is an imposter pretending to be the Self.

64.    The ego is the cause of all human sorrow and suffering.

65.    The ego is the cause of all disease, death, war, fear, anger and violence.

66.    Although many thousands of years have passed, human beings have made almost no inward progress toward ending suffering, sorrow, war, fear, anger, violence, cheating and lying.

67.    Thousands of years ago humans had suffering, sorrow, war, fear, anger, violence, cheating and lying.

68.    Now, today, currently, humans have suffering, sorrow, war, fear, anger, violence, cheating and lying.

69.    What has kept humans in the same pool of inward unsolved problems?

70.   The ego (the imposter) has kept humans in the same pool of inward unsolved problems.

71.   Inward problems cannot be solved by looking outward.

72.   Inward problems can only be solved by looking inward.

73.   The ego knows that if the attention is turned inward, the ego will be found to be a myth, an imposter, an illusion, a delusion, a dream.

74.   Therefore, due to the ego's fear of ending, the ego keeps the attention directed outward.

75.   Usually when people attempt to turn the attention inward, they are still looking outward because they do not understand the meaning of looking inward.

76.   All humans are slaves and the imposter "self" is their master.

77.   Exposing the strategies of that imposter "self", how to put an end to those strategies, how to bring the imposter "self" to an end, thus ending all suffering and sorrow and remaining in the true Self whose nature is infinite-eternal-awareness-love-bliss, are the primary purposes of this book.

78.   Ending the ego does not end the body.

79.   After the ego ends, the body will live out the natural course of its life.

80.   One should never attempt to harm the body.

81.　The ego is the "I thought."

82.　Ending the ego is ending the "I thought."

83.　Ending the bodily life will not end the ego.

84.　The ego will create the dream of a new body when the old body ends.

85.　Thus, ending the body does not help to solve the problems.

86.　Humans almost always have their attention directed outward towards thoughts, people, places, things, experiences, etc.

87.　The background of awareness is the true Self and humans almost always ignore it.

88.　Your true Self deserves your attention.

89.　When humans turn their attention away from thoughts, the body, the world, people, places, things, experiences, etc. and towards their awareness, eventually they will directly experience their true Self.

90.　The imposter (thought) pretending to be your self and calling its pretend self "I" should not be tolerated even for one moment.

91.　Especially an imposter that has created so much suffering and sorrow should not be tolerated even for one moment.

92.　The imposter (thought) is like a parasite.

93.  Because the ego believes it is a real entity, the ego is afraid of ending.

94.  The ego controls all thinking.

95.  Because the ego is afraid of ending and controls all thinking, the ego directs thought in ways that will preserve its imaginary self so that its imaginary self is not brought to an end.

96.  The purpose of the teachings in this book is to bring the imposter to an end so that what remains is only the true Self whose nature is infinite-eternal-awareness-bliss-love.

97.  When the imposter ends, all suffering and sorrow also end.

98.  Imagining that thinking or thought is your self is a delusion, a dreamlike illusion.

99.  Thinking that you are a body living in a world is a delusion, a dream-like illusion.

100.  Thought has created those delusions.

101.  All sorrow, suffering and delusions have one single root.

102.  The single root is thought.

103.  The root of thought is the "I thought."

104.  The root of thought is the thought "I."

105.  Thought is not part of your true nature.  Thought is something you learned.

106. Do not allow something you acquired to pretend to be your self.

107. Try this experiment: Set aside two hours when you have no other activities going on. Sit down in a place where you will not be disturbed. Shut your eyes. Make a decision that for the next two hours you will not allow a single thought to arise. If you are really in control of thinking, then not even one thought will arise. If thinking controls you, then even though you have made the decision not to allow a single thought to arise, you will not be able to sit for two hours without a single thought arising. What a revelation this can be to discover that thought, something that you acquired, now controls you.

108. Chapter One contains a description of the secret that has enslaved humanity for as long as there have been humans.


Read Chapter One very slowly three times before reading Chapter Two.

Note regarding other reasons for reading slowly and repetitively: People read spiritual books and various self-improvement books, sometimes hundreds of them without any change occurring in their lives. One of the reasons for this is that they are not familiar enough with the teachings for the teachings to have become tools they can use. In other words, the teachings have not really sunk in after a single reading. By reading one chapter three times before going unto the next chapter there is a much better chance of the teachings becoming a useable tool that can actually transform one's life. Since this book teaches what the ego would prefer to block out, this is even truer for this book.

# CHAPTER TWO

## THE IMPOSTER'S TRICKS

1.    The ego controls all thinking.

2.    The ego can create an argument against anything.

3.    Therefore, reserve all arguments against what is being presented here until you have read the book at least three times.

4.    Otherwise, the ego will generate arguments against any anti-ego presentation, thus blocking what is being presented.

5.    See the vicious circle:

6.    The ego in its attempts to prevent the ego from being exposed for the imposter that it is, and to block the realization that the ego is the cause of all human sorrow and suffering, creates arguments against what is revealed in this book.

7.    Because the ego sets the standards for the debate, the ego always wins the debate.

8.    The way to break that vicious circle is to delay all arguments against what is presented here until you have read the book very slowly at least three times.

9.    When the ego forms an argument against something in this book, see the argument as an ego preservation strategy and ignore it, postponing all argument until the presentation is complete.

10. Having the motivation to understand, instead of the motivation to argue, will help to produce an insight into what is being presented here.

11. Put the arguments on hold until you have read the book at least three times.

12. By that time you may be so skilled at recognizing the ego's preservation strategies, you may decide to delay the arguments forever.

13. At least give what is being presented here a fair chance by being aware of the arguments that the ego creates and disregarding those arguments until an insight into what is revealed here is awakened.

14. Plenty of time to argue later, after reading the entire book.

15. The ego has been deceiving humans for as long as there have been humans.

16. Be aware of the ego's attempts to deceive you.

17. The ego controls all thinking, therefore, various combinations of thoughts, ideas, beliefs and opinions are the ego's primary tools to preserve the ego's imaginary "self" and to prevent you from discovering your true Self.

18. Most humans have never observed the background of awareness, not even for one second.

19. Therefore, whatever opinions most people have about what the background of awareness is, what its qualities are, what the true Self is, etc., have no basis.

20.   If you observe the background of awareness for many hours every day, for a number of years, then you will eventually know that your awareness is infinite-eternal-awareness-love-bliss.

21.   Because most humans spend their entire lives looking outward at thoughts, the body, the world, people, places, things, etc., most humans never observe their own awareness, not even for one moment, in their entire lifetimes.

22.   Concepts, beliefs and conclusions are not truly important.   What is truly important is Direct Experience.

23.   Be aware of your thoughts, ideas, beliefs and opinions and see how they serve the ego.

24.   See Chapter One for a clarification of the difference between the ego and the true Self.

25.   This book is a practical guide to Direct Experience, not a theory for intellectual entertainment.

26.   Because the ego is afraid of ending, the ego directs and creates thoughts, ideas, concepts, beliefs and opinions that will help the ego to continue its illusion of being real and that will prevent the ego from being brought to an end.

27.   Those concepts are ego preservation strategies. Those concepts are the ego's tricks.

28.   Because thoughts can be combined in trillions of combinations, the ego can create trillions of preservation strategies.

29.   The ego has the ability to hide what it is doing from itself.

30.   The ego creates ego preservation strategies throughout the entire day.  Most people are not aware of the ego's preservation strategies.

31.   If you are not aware of how the ego preserves its imaginary self, then the ego succeeds in preserving its imaginary self.

32.   One of the purposes of this book is to look at how the ego preserves its imaginary self.

33.   If one million people study a spiritual teaching and only one of those people ends the ego illusion, why did the other nine hundred ninety-nine thousand, nine hundred ninety-nine miss the opportunity?

34.   The reason the other nine hundred ninety-nine thousand nine hundred ninety-nine people missed the opportunity is because of the ego's fear of ending.

35.   Due to the ego's fear of ending, the ego creates strategies to preserve its imaginary self.

36.   Distorting spiritual teachings is one of the many strategies the ego uses to preserve its imaginary self.

37.   That (#36 above) applies to the teachings in the book you are now reading and to all other spiritual teachings.

38.   Right from the beginning, the ego's preservation strategies have to be dealt with.

39.   If the ego's preservation strategies are not dealt with, the ego will block out or distort what is revealed in the book you are now reading.   Most attempts at awakening fail because of failure to put an end to the ego's preservation strategies.

40.   The ego's preservation strategies can be brought to an end.   We will look at how to do that in this book.

41.   Usually any mention of exposing the ego's preservation strategies makes the ego run the other way.

42.   Being willing to look at the ego's preservation strategies is a sign of spiritual maturity.

43.   Most people are not willing to look at the ego's preservation strategies.

44.   Reading a book that reveals some of the ego's preservation strategies will not make you immune to them.

45.   One of the ego's preservation strategies is the thought "This does not apply to me."

46.   The ego is very tricky and deceptive in all humans.   The ego is a liar in all humans.   The ego lies to its imaginary self.

47.   When something is pointed out in this book and you think "This does not apply to me," take a second look.

48.   Maybe it does apply to you and the ego is blocking that fact out as a preservation strategy.

49.    Challenge the thought "This does not apply to me."

50.    The thought "This does not apply to me" may be an ego preservation strategy.

51.    One of the differences between the one out of a million who awakens and the others who do not is the ability to stay focused on an essential point until it becomes an insight and a tool that you can use.

52.    An intellectual understanding of what is revealed in this book is only the first step.  The second step is to go beyond thought to awaken insight.

53.    The book you are now reading is filled with the insights that lay the foundation for you to be the one who awakens and not one of the millions who miss.

54.    Dwell on what is written in every sentence in every chapter until an insight is awakened that becomes a tool you can use.

55.    To awaken insight, don't read what is written here the way you read a newspaper or trivia, and don't read for the purpose of gathering information.

56.    To awaken insight, read as though you were reading instructions about how to fly that are vital to prevent you from crashing.

57.    Slowly reflect on each sentence.

58.    That is why the sentences are numbered with a space between them: to encourage you to reflect slowly on each sentence, to pause, and not to hurry to the next sentence.

59.   Continue to reread long after the intellect has understood the meaning of the words.

60.   Reading very, very slowly is insight reading.

61.   Read very slowly.   Then read at an even slower pace, allowing you to look deeply into each sentence, and to see what each sentence points towards.

62.   The ego is like an inchworm that lets go of one thought only when it has grabbed hold of the next thought.

63.   Therefore, when rereading every chapter many times over and over, don't be in a hurry to proceed to the next sentence.   Stay with each sentence for a long time before reading the next sentence.

64.   It is important to understand the difference between insight and intellectual understanding.

65.   Never confuse intellectual understanding with insight.

66.   Intellectual   understanding,   which   means understanding the words, is good as a first step.

67.   However, after one has understood the words, if one then goes on to another concept before the insight has awakened, the words may become obstacles and hindrances, instead of tools that end the ego.

68.   Intellectual   "understanding",   an   intellectual appetite and an intellectual approach to "spirituality" are what characterize the nine hundred ninety-nine thousand nine hundred ninety-nine who miss.

69.   Insight is the approach used by the one in a million who brings the ego to its final end.

70.   Most people study "spiritual" teachings because they enjoy the concepts.

71.   The ego is fundamentally dishonest in humans and the ego has the ability to hide what it is doing from its imaginary "self."

72.   Therefore, many people fail to see that their primary reason for studying "spiritual" teachings is because they enjoy the concepts.

73.   The desire to go quickly to the next concept and to gather more and more information and to read more and more spiritual books and to think about what has been read and to discuss what has been read and thought about, are symptoms of the intellectual appetite and intellectual "spirituality".

74.   Approaching the study of spiritual teachings intellectually, as just described (73), is an approach used by the nine hundred ninety-nine thousand nine hundred ninety-nine who miss.

75.   No opinions, philosophies or beliefs are presented in this book.

76.   The report of Direct Experience and a practical guide to Direct Experience are presented in the book you are now reading.

77.   Ideas are not what this book points towards.

78.   This book points towards the awareness that is prior to thought, and how to directly experience that awareness.

79.   The ego likes to scatter attention.

80.   Scattering attention is one of the ego's preservation strategies.

81.   Thinking scatters attention.

82.   To bring the attention to a single point and to dwell on that single point for a very long time is the way to awaken insight.

83.   Insight is not thinking and insight is not belief.

84.   Insight is a permanent new perspective.

85.   To find one powerful quote, not a quote that the spiritually immature ego selects in its efforts to preserve itself, and to stay with that quote until insight awakens, is the kind of approach used by the one in a million who brings the ego to its final end.

86.   One might stay with a single quote for one day or one week or much longer than one week.  Those who use this approach are rare.

87.   Keeping the attention directed outward is one of the ego's fundamental tricks.

88.   Creating unnecessary activities is one way the ego keeps the attention directed outward and is another of the ego's tricks.

89.    Dropping all unnecessary activities to create the maximum amount of time for spiritual practice is an essential key to success in bringing the ego to its final end.

90.    Pretending that a journey through thought is an authentic spiritual journey is also one of the ego's tricks.

91.    The ego has as many tricks to draw upon as there are concepts, ideas, beliefs and opinions.

92.    Choosing belief instead of Direct Experience is one of the ego's tricks.

93.    Wasting time is one of the ego's tricks.

94.    Spending time in entertainment that could have been spent in spiritual practice is one of the ego's tricks.

95.    Almost all thoughts are just the ego's tricks.

96.    Reflect on one sentence for a very long time before reading the next sentence.

97.    Reflecting means looking.

98.    Reflecting does not mean thinking and reflecting does not mean arguing.

99.    Stay with each sentence until you have an insight into it.

100. The previous sentence (99) describes a key approach used by the one in a million who succeeds in living in infinite-eternal-awareness-love-bliss.

101. There are a few key principles to be understood and a little reading may be required for that.

102. However, to go on and on reading more and more spiritual books, one after another, is an ego preservation strategy; another trick the ego uses.

103. Most reading, discussing and thinking about spiritual teachings are ego preservation strategies (tricks created by the ego to preserve its imaginary self).

104. The ego continues thinking about spiritual concepts to avoid the practice that leads to the ego's final end.

105. The ego keeps people lost in an endless maze of concepts.

106. Spiritual concepts do not lead to freedom.

107. Only practice leads to freedom.

108. However, it must be the most rapid and direct spiritual practice and not a practice created by or distorted by the ego.

Read Chapter Two very slowly three times before reading Chapter Three.

# CHAPTER THREE

# THE IMPOSTER'S TOOLS:

# THOUGHT, THINKING AND BELIEFS

1.    Thought is the primary tool the ego uses to preserve its imaginary self.

2.    Therefore, it is important to see how the ego uses thought to create ego preservation strategies.

3.    First one must understand the nature of thinking, thought, concepts and beliefs and the myths the ego has created about thinking, thought, concepts and beliefs.

4.    Thought is not a means to discover the absolute Truth.

5.    The ego has convinced almost all humans and almost all spiritual aspirants that thought is a means to know the absolute Truth.

6.    Some people think they already know that thought is not a means to know the absolute Truth.

7.    Almost all of those people are still trying to use thought as a means to know the absolute Truth.

8.    This reveals that they do not really know that thought is not a means to know the absolute Truth.

9.    They have confused knowing-insight-awareness with conceptual "knowing."

10.    People tend to believe in thought.

11.    Thinking is controlled by the ego and the ego uses thought to preserve its imaginary self.

12.    Therefore, to believe in thoughts, ideas and concepts, including those thoughts that people imagine are their own thoughts, is an error that results in failure to end the ego.

13.    Thoughts, ideas, beliefs, concepts, emotions and desires are the fundamental tools the imposter self (ego) uses to prevent you from directly experiencing your True Self.

14.    For those few individuals who are seriously intent on liberation, it is essential to stop using thought as a means to know the absolute Truth.

15.    It is also essential to stop believing in thoughts, ideas, and concepts; including those thoughts, ideas and concepts you imagine being your own.

16.    Understanding the nature of beliefs can help one to see that thought is not a means to know the absolute Truth.

17.    Seeing that thought is not a means to know the absolute Truth is the way to stop using thought as a means to know the absolute Truth.

18.    There is a method you can try that reveals that thought is not a means to know the absolute Truth.

19.    It is the "How Do You Know Method."

20. Here are the instructions for the How Do You Know Method (21-27):

21. Look at any belief you have.

22. Ask of that belief, "How do I know absolutely for sure this is true?"

23. The mind will give an answer.

24. To the answer the mind gives ask "How do I know absolutely for sure this is true?"

25. Every time the mind gives an answer, question the answer by repeating the question "How do I know absolutely for sure this is true?"

26. You must be willing to question every answer the mind gives for the method to work.

27. If you are willing to question every answer the mind gives to the question "How do I know absolutely for sure this is true?" the inquiry will always end in "I don't know absolutely for sure this is true".

28. The How Do You Know Method is an excellent way to see the difference between believing and knowing.

29. The How Do You Know Method is also an excellent way to see that thought is not a means to know the absolute Truth.

30. After questioning a few hundred beliefs using the How Do You Know Method, it should be quite clear that thought is not a means to know the absolute Truth.

31.  Thought is like a great pretense or house of cards.

32.  One idea is supported by another idea.

33.  The How Do You Know Method is a way to see that when you trace each idea back, you find there is actually no real foundation at all.

34.  There is another way to see that thought is not a way to know the absolute Truth: understand the nature of belief and concepts; see how belief is formed and how the ego creates ideas that preserve its imaginary self.

35.  It is the "Arguing Both Sides Method".

36.  The Arguing Both Sides Method begins by looking at some belief you have, maybe one of the current issues of the day.

37.  Write an argument for your belief.

38.  Look at your belief and write up all the proofs, arguments, evidence, and reasons that support it.

39.  Next, pretend that you have the opposite belief and write up all the proofs, arguments, evidence and reasons that support that opposite belief.

40.  The purpose of the Arguing Both Sides Method is to demonstrate that thought can create reasons, evidence and support for any belief.

41.  Seeing that thought can create evidence and reasons to support any belief, is a very powerful key.

42.    The Arguing Both Sides Method is another way of revealing that thought is really baseless.

43.    The    Arguing    Both    Sides    Method    also demonstrates that thought forms conclusions based on motive.

44.    Evidence    is    not    the    primary    factor    that determines what conclusions and beliefs will be formed.

45.    Motivation is the primary factor in the forming of beliefs.

46.    Evidence will be gathered to support the motive.

47.    The ego will gather all the so-called evidence and reasons to support what the ego wants to believe.

48.    The ego's primary motive is to preserve its imaginary self.

49.    Therefore, the ego directs thought to create concepts that will help to preserve its imaginary self.

50.    In almost all humans, including almost all spiritual aspirants and students, the desire of the ego to preserve its imaginary self is very strong.

51.    In almost all humans including almost all spiritual aspirants and students, the ego directs thought to create concepts that will preserve its imaginary self.

52.    One of the ego's preservation strategies is selecting spiritual paths that are not direct.

53.   Even if one manages to find the Direct Path, the ego will distort the Direct Path by interpreting what is written or said in a way that supports the ego, or the ego will distort the Direct Path by focusing on that which is not essential.

54.   One of the tricks (ego preservation strategies) that the ego uses most commonly with spiritual aspirants is to confuse intellectual "spirituality" with authentic spirituality.

55.   Most people only have an intellectual interest in spiritual concepts and do not wish to end the ego.

56.   Most people just enjoy learning about the concepts.

57.   There are some people who realize their interest is only intellectual.

58.   There are other people who believe they have an interest in ending the ego, who do not really have an interest in ending the ego.

59.   Almost all of the people on a spiritual path that claims to have as its aim the ending of the ego illusion, have very little desire to end the ego illusion.

60.   The way to end all of the ego's preservation strategies is to increase the desire for liberation.

61.   There are a few very condensed Direct Path teachings that can be a great help on the Direct Path.

62.   You will find those Direct Path teachings in the book you are now reading.

63. However, to go on and on reading books and discussing spiritual teachings is an ego preservation strategy to keep you in the realm of thought instead of practice.

64. All of the time you spend reading and discussing could be better spent in practice.

65. Practice leads to liberation.

66. Endless reading and discussing leads to illusion.

67. The ego creates arguments against the Direct Path as a preservation strategy.

68. The ego calls indirect paths "direct paths" as an ego preservation strategy.

69. Instead of spending all one's spare time in spiritual practice, the ego finds almost endless ways to spend one's spare time, and this is one of the ego's primary preservation strategies. Some examples are television, entertainment, reading, discussing, and thinking. The ego can find thousands of ways to avoid spiritual practice.

70. If you drop all your unnecessary activities, you will have much more time for spiritual practice.

71. One ego preservation strategy (one of the imposter's tricks) is creating arguments against what is written here instead of open-mindedly considering the possibility that what is revealed in this book points towards the truth that the ego prevents most people from seeing.

72.   Another ego preservation strategy (trick the imposter uses) is deciding in advance that one of the methods will not work, without ever giving the method a sincere try.

73.   See how the ego directs every thought to create a way to preserve its imaginary self.

74.   In other words, ask of every thought, idea, concept, belief, etc.: "Does this thought, idea, concept or belief help the ego illusion to continue?"

75.   When you form a belief, you are no closer to discovering the absolute Truth than you were before you formed the belief.

76.   When you form a belief, you have created an obstacle to discovering the absolute Truth.

77.   If you were honest, instead of a belief, your view would be "I don't know."

78.   If you really wanted Truth, you would insist on Direct Experience.

79.   If you really wanted Truth, you would never accept a belief.  A belief is only a group of symbols.  All words are symbols.

80.   The extremely intense desire for liberation is the key to ending the ego's tricks, and the book you are now reading contains step-by-step instructions for awakening the extremely intense desire for liberation.

81.   This book exposes some of the strategies the ego uses to preserve its imaginary self.

82.    Reading this book is a good first step.

83.    Repeated reading, over and over, reflecting on each sentence, is very important.  If at some point in the future you have dropped all unnecessary activities and are using all of the free time thus created to practice the Awareness Watching Awareness Method, then your time will be far better spent in practice instead of reading.  However, in the beginning, most people need a foundation to motivate them to drop all unnecessary activities and to practice, and thus in the beginning reading this book is very important.

84.    Your motivation while reading is very important.

85.    The correct motivations are (86-89):

86.    Extremely intense Self-honesty.

87.    An extremely intense desire to directly experience the infinite-eternal-absolute Truth.

88.    A willingness to let go of all the ideas you have accumulated in the past.

89.    An extremely intense longing to be free of sorrow and to live in eternal-joy.

90.    If the extremely intense desire for liberation is awakened in you, the clarity, honesty, insight, integrity and earnestness that the extremely intense desire for liberation brings, will not allow the desire for liberation to become weak again.

91.    If the desire for Liberation becomes weak, it means that the extremely intense desire for Liberation has not yet been awakened in you.

92.    When the extremely intense desire for Freedom is awakened, clarity, sincerity, earnestness, insight and discernment are also awakened, and then you can see what is essential and what is not essential.

93.    The end of the ego is the end of all suffering and all sorrow for all eternity.

94.    The end of the ego is infinite-eternal-awareness-love-bliss.

95.    Realize that ending the ego is the only truly worthwhile event that can happen in a human life.

96.    Take a look at your actions moment by moment to see if they conform to the realization that ending the ego is the only truly valuable event that can happen in a human life.

97.    The ego projects thoughts and fantasies and the ego interprets.

98.    One way to stop this distortion is to ask, "Is this thought I am having about what I am reading, really in the words I am reading, or have I added a thought that is not there in the words I am reading?"

99.    Another way to stop the distortion is to ask, "Have I added a concept or interpretation to what I am reading?"

100. Most people project much thinking onto the teachings that they read.

101. Their thinking has very little to do with the teachings they have read.

102. Almost all humans are in a state of chaotic confusion.

103. Most people do not realize that they are in a state of chaotic confusion.

104. Interpreting what is written is an expression of that chaotic confusion.

105. Actually practicing #98 and #99 (on page 38) can help greatly to end that distortion.

106. Awakening the extremely intense desire for liberation will stop the ego from creating ego preservation strategies.

107. Chapter Four is about the importance of awakening the extremely intense desire for liberation.

108. Read Chapter Three very slowly three times before reading Chapter Four.

## CHAPTER FOUR

## THE DESIRE FOR LIBERATION

1.    Awakening the extremely intense desire for Liberation is the most important first step that can be taken towards being liberated now in this lifetime.

2.    The extremely intense desire for liberation is (3-7):

3.    The extremely intense desire for the direct experience of the absolute Truth.

4.    The extremely intense longing for the ending of sorrow and the experience of eternal-love-joy.

5.    The extremely intense desire to experience who or what you really are at your core and to live eternally as your true Self.

6.    The extremely intense desire for freedom from all illusion and delusion and freedom from the ego which is the source of all illusion and delusion.

7.    The extremely intense desire to awaken from the human nightmare.

8.    The extremely intense desire for liberation is the foundation of all true spirituality.

9.    Of all of the factors that determine if you will or will not be free, the intensity or lack of intensity of your desire for liberation is the most essential factor.

10.    Whatever you can do to most effectively increase your desire for liberation should be done.

11.   Spiritual teachings are not all equal.

12.   Some teachings are essential powerful keys.

13.   The knowledge that increasing your desire for Liberation is the most effective first step you can take is an essential powerful key.

14.   All obstacles that appear in your journey to Freedom are caused by too little desire for Freedom.

15.   Even a little increase in your desire for Freedom is helpful.

16.   As your desire for Freedom grows in intensity, the ego creates fewer obstacles.

17.   When your desire for Freedom becomes very intense, your desire for Freedom demands that you take no detours.

18.   When your desire for Freedom becomes extremely intense, for the first time you can see what is essential for Freedom and what is not essential.

19.   When your desire for Freedom is weak, the ego does not allow you to see its preservation strategies.

20.   When the desire for Freedom is stronger, you can begin to see the ego's preservation strategies.

21.   When the desire for Freedom becomes even stronger, the desire for Freedom itself will bring you everything you need to succeed in your quest for Liberation including the answer to all your questions, the Direct Path teachings, the solution to all obstacles, the motivation to practice, etc.

22.   You will be able to see how before the awakening of the extremely intense desire for Liberation, the ego selected spiritual teachings that would help to preserve the ego.

23.   When the desire for Freedom becomes even more intense you can see all of the ego's preservation strategies.

24.   When the extremely intense desire for Liberation is awakened you will marvel at how it was possible you did not see the ego's preservation strategies before.

25.   When the extremely intense desire for Liberation is awakened, you will be able to see how the ego distorted even the Direct Path teachings.

26.   When the extremely intense desire for Liberation is awakened, you will be able to see that every spiritual teaching from the past has been distorted by the ego and that some of the spiritual teachings were created by the ego for the purpose of preserving the ego.

27.   When the extremely intense desire for Liberation is awakened, you will be able to see that almost all of the spiritual and religious teachings of the past are distractions and detours that serve the ego.

28.   When the extremely intense desire for Liberation is awakened, you will be surprised at how little the ego let you see before.

29.   When the extremely intense desire for Liberation is awakened, you will see the endless maze of concepts the ego created to trap your attention.

30.   When the desire for Freedom becomes even more intense, the ego will no longer create ego preservation strategies.

31.   The extremely intense desire for the direct experience of the absolute Truth will guide you to your inner Teacher.

32.   The extremely intense desire for Truth will guide you to the practice that gives the direct experience of Eternal Life.

33.   The key is the intensity of the desire for the direct experience of the absolute Truth.

34.   Increasing your desire for the Truth is the most important first step.

35.   Increasing your desire for Freedom is essential.

36.   Without an increase in your desire for Freedom, all of your attempts at awakening will fail to produce the Eternal Experience.

37.   Without an increase in your desire for Freedom, the ego will distort all of your spiritual studies, including what you read in this book.

38.   Without an increase in your desire for Freedom, the ego will never allow you to see the Truth.

39.   Another great key is Self-honesty.

40.   Self-honesty will help in all aspects of the quest for Liberation.

41.   Self-honesty will help you increase your desire for Liberation.

42.   Self-honesty is being as honest as you can be.

43.   Self-honesty means to be 100% honest with your Self, all the time.

44.   Catch your ego using ego preservation strategies.

45.   See your ego creating arguments that lead you away from the Direct Path.

46.   What if your desire for Liberation were to double from its present level?

47.   If your desire for Liberation were to double from its present level, that would be a huge help.

48.   If your desire for Liberation were to double from its present level, immediately you would begin to see what you have never been able to see before.

49.   What if your desire for Liberation were a million times greater and more intense than it is now?

50.   Really, even if your desire for Liberation doubles or triples, great changes will occur in what the ego allows you to see.

51.   When your desire for Liberation increases greatly, every moment of your life will be dedicated to your Liberation.

52. That great intense desire for Liberation will demand that you do not waste even one moment of time, that you stop the ego lies, and that you drop that which is not essential.

53. The wonderful thing is, that same extreme desire for Liberation that brings you the knowledge of what is essential and what is not essential, also allows you to see for the first time in your life.

54. Before the extremely intense desire for Freedom arises, you think you can see, but really you are blind.

55. After the extremely intense desire for Freedom arises all is made clear and you have no doubts!

56. After the extremely intense desire for Freedom arises, for the first time you can see!

57. If the extremely intense desire for Liberation does **not** arise in you (58-62):

58. The words in this book will be of little or no real benefit to you.

59. The ego will interpret what is written here in the book you are now reading.

60. The ego will create arguments against what is written here.

61. Instead of seeing what you read literally, without any interpretation, the ego will begin to interpret.

62. The ego will change the teachings into something that preserves the ego instead of something that brings the ego to its final end.

63. Therefore, the most essential key is to awaken the extremely intense desire for Liberation and to make that desire for Freedom grow every day.

64. One of the most powerful tools or keys you can have is to change the way you read.

65. Read extremely slowly, reflecting on a single phrase or a single sentence.

66. Make sure you see the meaning of the sentence before proceeding to the next sentence.

67. When reading: pause, stop and look.

68. Read the same verse three times before proceeding to the next verse.

69. If the desire for Freedom is not great enough in you, the ego will always find a way to occupy your time with something other than spiritual practice.

70. Thus the key to bringing the ego to an end is the intensity of the desire for Freedom.

71. Imagine someone being held underwater. How eager is he to rise to the surface to breathe air?

72. Your desire for Liberation must be as intense as that man's desire for air.

73. Freedom must be as high on your list of priorities as air is on that man's list of priorities.

74. How great and how intense is the desire for air for someone being held underwater?

75.   He would like to rise to the surface, but he is being held underwater.

76.   See how intense his desire is to rise to the surface so he can breathe air.

77.   Every second his desire to rise to the surface becomes more and more intense.

78.   After one minute underwater, his desire to breathe is much more intense.

79.   After two minutes underwater, his desire to rise to the surface for oxygen is ten times greater.

80.   After three minutes underwater, his desire to rise to the surface is one hundred times greater.

81.   After four minutes underwater, his desire to rise to the surface is one thousand times greater.

82.   How great and how intense is his desire?

83.   That is how great and how intense your desire for Liberation must become, if you are going to succeed in your quest for Eternal Freedom.

84.   If the extremely intense desire for Freedom is not present, you can always find a way to avoid spiritual practice.

85.   If the extremely intense desire for Freedom is not present, there is almost no limit to the ego's capacity to distort.

86. Suppose there was a book written by an awakened sage that was one thousand pages long and the only words that were written were the following identical words repeated on every page (87-93):

87. The only effective means to end the ego illusion is to (88-93):

88. Turn your attention *away* from thought, the body, the world, people, places, things, experiences, etc., and turn your attention *towards* awareness watching awareness.

89. If through other means you attempt to bring the ego to an end, the ego may appear to have ended; however, eventually the ego will reappear.

90. Therefore, there are no other effective means to end the ego, to end all suffering and all sorrow, and to live eternally as infinite-awareness-love-bliss.

91. Start by setting aside at least two hours per day, with no other activities, for your practice of awareness watching awareness.

92. If by dropping unnecessary activities you can create more than two hours for practice, do so.

93. Set aside as many hours per day as you can spare to practice awareness watching awareness, with no other activities occurring during your practice time.

94. Even if the above verses (87-93) were written on every page, most people would not put into practice the instructions given in those verses.

95.   Most people would not put the instructions into practice because their desire for Liberation is not strong enough.

96.   The desire to preserve the ego is much greater than the desire to end the ego.  This is true for almost all humans and almost all spiritual aspirants.

97.   The ego has trillions of tricks to preserve its imaginary self.

98.   To the previously quoted passages (87-93), the aspirant might say (99-103):

99.   "He does not really mean the only effective means."

100.  "He does not really mean we need to set aside time with no other activities."

101.  "He does not really mean we need to practice."

102.  "The book is actually written in code."

103.  "There are deeper, hidden, subtle meanings that are more important."

104.  If this (99-103) seems insane to you, you are correct, it is insane.

105.  The word "insane" describes well almost all humans.

106.  They may not use those exact words (99-103) to distort and complicate.

107. They will find their own words to distort and complicate. 99-103 are examples of how people can distort the teachings. The truth is he really does mean the only effective means; and that time must be set aside for practice with no other activities; and that you need to practice. He really wrote in plain words without a code; and he really wanted you to take the words literally without searching for hidden meanings.

108. The only cure for all this is the awakening of the extremely intense desire for Freedom.

109. What if your present desire for Freedom were to become a million times more intense than it is now? (110-114):

110. Then there would not be time for all these games, detours, distractions, delays and distortions.

111. Then you would stop listening to teachers who are supposedly liberated but who are not liberated.

112. Then you would not pretend that thinking about spirituality is authentic Spirituality.

113. Then you would not pretend that an intellectual journey is a Spiritual journey.

114. Then the only means you would accept is the most direct means.

115. Then you would be just like the man who is being held underwater trying to rise up for air (116-127):

116. He does not have time for discussion.

117. He does not have time for games.

118. He does not have time for false teachers.

119. He does not have time for indirect methods.

120. He does not have time for endless reading.

121. He does not have time for television.

122. He does not have time for projecting an imagined meaning onto the teachings.

123. He does not have time for entertainment.

124. He does not have time for pretending to want to be free.

125. He does not have time for any dishonesty with himself.

126. He does not have time for pretending he has risen to the surface.

127. He does not have time for any debate or argument.

128. The only thing he has time for is to focus all of his attention on rising to the surface.

129. That is why the most important key is the intensity of the desire for Freedom.

130. The only problem an aspirant ever has is a desire for Liberation that is too weak. An extremely intense desire for Liberation will solve all the other problems.

Read Chapter Four very slowly three times before reading Chapter Five.

# CHAPTER FIVE

# HOW TO AWAKEN

# THE EXTREMELY INTENSE

# DESIRE FOR LIBERATION

1.   The primary means to awaken the extremely intense desire for Liberation is to carefully examine the two choices every day until the extremely intense desire for Freedom awakens.

2.   Choice A is to choose to end the ego by dropping all unnecessary activities to create the maximum amount of time every day to practice the most direct and rapid means to eternal bliss.

3.   The most direct and rapid means to eternal bliss is the Awareness Watching Awareness Method described in Chapter Seven.

4.   Choice A is Infinite-Eternal-Awareness-Love-Bliss with no sorrow and no suffering.

5.   Choice A is Eternal Life.

6.   Choice A is to live as your true Self forever.

7.   Choice A is absolutely perfect joy.

8.   The above (2-7) is a summary of Choice A.

9.   Some people may find it helpful to read more descriptions of Choice "A" written by the Awakened Ones who have taught in the past.

For more information about where such descriptions can be read go to this website: www.seeseer.com

10.    Choice B is being identified with a body subject to suffering, disease, death, violence, anger, fear, etc.

11.    Choice B is to allow an imposter called the ego to pretend to be yourself and to control you.

12.    Choice B is to allow an imposter (ego) that has created all the wars, diseases, death, suffering and evil that every human has ever experienced, to continue.

13.    Choice B is to have a temporary and therefore futile life that leads only to death.  That (10-13) is a summary of Choice B.

14.    In order to better examine Choice B you can make a list of all the forms that human suffering takes.

15.    You can write on that list thousands of wars; thousands of diseases; thousands of forms of violence; all of the ways that humans deceive, hurt, and cheat each other; and every other form of human suffering that you can think of.  Usually humans look at only a small part of the ocean of human suffering.  The purpose of the list is to look at the entire ocean of human suffering and the entire negative side of human life in a single glance. The purpose of the list is to see the consequences of choosing B.

16.    You need only read the suffering list once.

17.    After that, repeated reading of the summaries of choices A and B in Chapter Five should be enough.

18. Read Chapter Five every day comparing the summary of Choice A and the summary of Choice B until the extremely intense desire for Liberation awakens in you.

19. Read Chapter Five everyday until you Choose A.

20. An aid to awakening the extremely intense desire for Liberation is to see the value of the Eternal and the futility of the temporary. The ego leads humans throughout their lives from one temporary trivial pursuit to another temporary trivial pursuit. To see the pointlessness of the temporary and the great value of the eternal can be a great help. If you look into the future to see where all these trivial pursuits and useless activities will lead in the end, that also can be a great aid in revealing the pointlessness of the temporary. Ask of each activity and each moment, "What does this lead to?", and after that "Then what?" and later, "What will this finally lead to in the end?"

21. Often remembering that the body can end at any moment can also help to awaken the extremely intense desire for Freedom. Living every day as though it is your last day, using each precious moment to prepare for the Eternal, can also be a great help. Imagine there are two businesses you could invest in. You can see that a wrecking ball is about to destroy the first business. You can see that the second business will last forever. The obvious wise choice is to invest in the business that will last forever.

22. How will you know you have made Choice A? When you drop all unnecessary activities every day and use all of that free time to practice every day the most direct and rapid means to eternal bliss.

23.  How will you know the extremely intense desire for Liberation has been awakened?  When you drop all unnecessary activities every day and use all of the free time thus created to actually practice every day the most direct and rapid means to eternal bliss, you will know the extremely intense desire for Freedom has been awakened.

24.  The Awakening of the extremely intense desire for Liberation, which can also be called "really making Choice A," is (25-55):

25.  It is like a sign a trillion miles high stating NO MORE.

26.  NO MORE to all of the human evils of the past.

27.  NO MORE to all of the horrors the ego has created.

28.  It is like a silent shout saying NO MORE so loudly that if it were given a voice it would shatter the eardrums of every human on earth.

29.  It is a demand for Truth.

30.  It is the absolute demand for absolute Truth.

31.  It is the absolute demand for the final end of all human opinions.

32.  It is the absolute demand for absolute goodness.

33.  It is the absolute demand for the final end of the imposter who is called ego.

34. It is the absolute demand for the Direct Experience of the true Self.

35. It is like an infinitely strong grip that grabs hold of Truth with a power so strong nothing can weaken it.

36. It is like an infinitely strong grip that grabs hold of the true Self with such strength, nothing is powerful enough to weaken that grip.

37. The extremely intense desire for Liberation is like an infinitely strong grip that grabs hold of the absolute goodness that has never known falsehood with a hold so strong that nothing can weaken that grip.

38. It is like an absolutely immovable "NO" saying no to the trillions of human lies spoken in the past and the billions of human lies being thought of each day.

39. It is like an absolute "NO" to the trillions of horrors humans have created in the past and the billions of horrors humans are creating every day.

40. It is an absolute demand for the end of all sorrow and suffering.

41. It is an absolute demand for perfect infinite-eternal-love-joy.

42. It is an absolute demand that the source of all suffering, violence and evil, which is the imposter called ego, comes to a final end.

43. It is an absolute devotion to the true Self that is the background of awareness.

44.   That absolute devotion is turning the attention away from the world, the body, thought, etc., and towards awareness watching awareness.

45.   The extremely intense desire for Liberation is a demand for Truth that never compromises.

46.   It is a demand for the end of thought.

47.   It is a demand for the direct experience of the absolute Truth.

48.   When the extremely intense desire for Freedom arises, these demands are directed inwards, not towards others.

49.   When the extremely intense desire for Freedom arises, one never again bows before any egotistical human.

50.   When the extremely intense desire for Freedom arises, all obstacles are swept away.

51.   The extremely intense desire for Freedom is absolute dedication and devotion to the absolute Truth.

52.   It is absolute dedication and devotion to knowing the true Self in direct experience.

53.   After the extremely intense desire for Liberation is awakened, every moment of one's life is dedicated to awakening from the human dream.

54.   When the extremely intense desire for Liberation is awakened, all of the ego's lies, tricks, deceptions and games are seen for what they are and all of the ego's lies, tricks, deceptions and games eventually end.

55. When the extremely intense desire for Liberation is awakened, the nightmare the ego has created is no longer tolerated.

56. The ego is the source of all evil.

57. The ego is insane. This is true for all humans.

58. To produce so many trillions of horrors, the ego has to be evil and insane.

59. Something in you longs for an end to the imposter's dream.

60. Something in you longs for infinite Love.

61. Something in you longs for the end of all suffering and sorrow.

62. Something in you longs for eternal-joy-love.

63. It is possible to end the ego's dream and to discover the true Self which is free of all suffering and whose nature is infinite-eternal-love-joy.

64. It is possible in this lifetime while this body is living.

65. Cooperate with your Heart.

66. Stop listening to your ego.

67. If you turn your attention away from thought and towards awareness watching awareness and sustain that look for many hours every day, eventually the ego dream will end and the true Self will be experienced.

68.     Then all suffering ends and what remains is the eternal perfection of awareness-love-bliss.

69.     Make Choice A.

70.     Make your choice absolute and absolutely immovable.

71.     Make your choice absolutely solid and final.

72.     Your true Self, the background of awareness that is looking through your eyes, deserves your attention.

73.     For your entire life, you have been ignoring your true Self.

74.     Your true Self, the background of awareness, deserves your love and attention.

75.     Demand sanity.

76.     The human dream is insane.

77.     Demand sanity by waking up from the human dream into the reality of your own awareness.

78.     Make Choice A by dropping all unnecessary activities to create more time for spiritual practice.

79.     Make Choice A by dropping all distractions, detours and entertainment to create more time every day for spiritual practice.

80.     Make Choice A by making sure your practice is the most direct and rapid means to eternal bliss.

81.    The suffering that life brings is also a means to awaken the extremely intense desire for Liberation.

82.    Reading Chapter Five everyday is a much easier and more rapid means to awaken the extremely intense desire for Freedom.

83.  Some people will have an insight that permanently awakens the extremely intense desire for Freedom.

84.    However, for most people the awakening of the extremely intense desire for Freedom is a daily battle, with the intensity of the desire for Freedom fluctuating.

Read Chapter Five very slowly at least three times before reading Chapter Six.

# CHAPTER SIX

# THE

# AWARENESS WATCHING AWARENESS

## DISCOVERY

1.   By the year 2001 the author of the book you are now reading had been studying the teachings of almost all of the various religions and spiritual paths for 27 years.

2.   He had read more than two thousand spiritual books.

3.   He had received instruction from many spiritual teachers in America and India.

4.   It was clear that the essence of most spiritual teachings was focusing the attention on the "I AM."

5.   The place where "Hinduism," Buddhism, Judaism, Christianity and Islam meet is turning inward and focusing the attention on "I AM."

6.   The most direct and rapid means to eternal bliss, finding the kingdom within, "Self-Realization," Nirvana, etc., is turning the attention within to focus on "I AM."

7.   One modern example of this in "Hinduism" is Sri Nisargadatta Maharaj.

8.   Nisargadatta's teacher (guru) told him to pay attention to the "I AM" to the exclusion of all else.

9.     Nisargadatta practiced focusing his attention on the "I AM" for three years.

10.     After three years of practicing in his spare time, Nisargadatta realized his true Self.

11.     Nisargadatta had to work to support his family; therefore, he could only practice in his spare time.  He spent hours each day looking at the true Self.

12.     Focusing the attention on "I AM," excluding all else from one's attention, is an ancient "Hindu" practice.

13.     In Zen Buddhism focusing the attention on "who is looking" is found in the teachings of Master Bassui and the ancient Zen text *The Ceasing of Notions*.  In Tibetan Buddhism focusing attention on awareness is found in some of the Dzogchen practice instructions.

14.     The importance of looking inward and knowing the "I AM" is also found in the Judeo-Christian teachings (15-19):

15.     "And God said to Moses, I AM THAT I AM.  And He said Thus you shall say to the children of Israel, I AM has sent me to you." (Exodus 3:14)

16.     "Be still and know I AM God." (Psalm 46:10)

17.     The entire book *The Impersonal Life*, a book of Christian Mysticism, is written around the single verse "Be still and know I AM God." (Psalm 46:10)

18.     "Jesus said, Before Abraham was, I AM." (John 8:58)

19.   "Jesus said, The Kingdom of God is within you." (Luke 17:21)

20.   Jesus did **not** say, "Will be within you after your body dies."

21.   Jesus said "is." "Is" is present tense. "Is" is now.

22.   The Prophet Mohammad said, "He who knows his Self knows his Lord." Self-Cognition is a Sufi practice.

23.   There are many other spiritual traditions and teachings that have pointed out that focusing the attention on the "I AM" is the most direct and rapid means to Freedom (i.e. Know thyself).

24.   Another modern example from "Hinduism" is Sri Ramana Maharshi.

25.   Ramana Maharshi taught for more than 50 years that the only effective means to end the ego and suffering and to remain as eternal joy is to focus on the Self, the I, the I AM.

26.   By the year 2001, the author of the book you are now reading had attempted to practice the method of focusing the attention on the "I AM" for 27 years.

27.   The author had made very little progress with that method or any other method.

28.   In December of 2001 the author was in Tiruvannamalai, India for the purpose of attending the talks of a teacher in the Ramana Maharshi tradition.

29.   The author was alone in a room at the Sesha Bhavan guesthouse.

30.   The author was thinking about all the possible meanings of "I" and "I AM" and all the possible approaches to "I" and "I AM" that he had read about over the years:

31.   The "I thought," the thought I AM.

32.   The "I feeling," the feeling I AM.

33.   The "I consciousness," the "I AM" consciousness.

34.   To think I or I AM.

35.   To feel I or I AM.

36.   To focus the attention on I or I AM.

37.   Many different combinations of approaches and the different views of what "I" or "I AM" means.

38.   After 27 years, the author was still not sure what "I AM" means in direct experience.

39.   The author was wondering if there was some way to solve these questions and to have clarity both in the meaning of I or I AM and how to approach it; whether to focus the attention on I AM, or feel I AM, or think I AM, or...?

40.   The author wanted an understanding that was so clear, there would be nothing vague remaining, no more choices remaining.

41.   The author really wanted to know the answer.

42.    The author was not going to confine the answer to any previous understanding.

43.    The author was willing to have his previous understanding shattered, if necessary.

44.    There was a willingness to consider the possibility that for the last two and a half decades, the author had not understood at all what the "I AM" is or how to focus on it.

45.    It was a willingness to allow all the old views to be swept away, if necessary.

46.    Ramana Maharshi had said Self-inquiry is more like feeling than like thought.

47.    Asking "Who am I?" or asking "To whom do these thoughts arise?" are easy instructions to follow as long as one stays in the realm of thought.

48.    However, when it comes to feeling "Who am I?" or feeling "I AM," the instructions had always been a bit vague.  What exactly is the feeling I AM?

49.    How do I know I AM?

50.    Nisargadatta Maharaj and many others had said the "I AM" is consciousness.

51.    The author wondered: "is the 'I AM' the 'I thought' or is the 'I AM' just my present awareness?"

52.    The author thought: "if the 'I AM' is this present awareness, the awareness that is now looking at this room, then paying attention to the 'I AM' is just" (53):

53.   **My awareness watching my awareness.**

54.   This was a revelation!

55.   Instead of having some vague practice where one is told to pay attention to the "I AM" without ever being sure exactly what the "I AM" is and feels like, here was an absolutely clear instruction:   **My present awareness watching my present awareness**.

56.   Not some unknown, seemingly far away awareness labeled the Infinite Self or labeled God.

57.   This awareness, my awareness, here and now watching itself, while ignoring thought, the body, the world, etc.

58.   Immediately the author tried this practice (59-65):

59.   Turning the attention away from thought and towards awareness watching awareness.

60.   The author shut his eyes, because the point was also to ignore the world.

61.   To turn the attention that normally goes out into the world around 180 degrees and to look inward.

62.   To turn the attention *away from* thoughts, feelings and desires and *towards* awareness watching awareness.

63.   If the author noticed a thought, he ignored the thought and brought the attention back to awareness watching awareness.

64. Awareness paying attention to awareness to the exclusion of all else.

65. Awareness paying attention only to itself.

66. The results were instant!

67. From the very first moment one tries this practice, one is abiding as awareness!

68. There is no waiting!

69. It is easy.

70. This is not meant to imply that from the beginning the ego ends.

71. It takes years of continuous practice before the ego meets its final end.

72. However, from the moment one tries this easy to understand practice, one is being as awareness!

73. The author practiced the Awareness Watching Awareness Method for two years, from December 2001 to January 2004.

74. There were more days with twelve hours of practice than days with two hours of practice.

75. In January of 2004 the author's ego, sorrow and suffering came to its final end, and what remained is *Infinite-Eternal-Awareness-Love-Bliss*.

76. Thus the Awareness Watching Awareness Method once again lived up to its reputation as being the most direct and rapid means to eternal bliss in this lifetime.

77.   Ramana Maharshi and Nisargadatta Maharaj had both specifically described the Awareness Watching Awareness Method; however, the author's ego did not allow him to pay attention to those quotes.

78.   The Awareness Watching Awareness Method was like a buried treasure, hidden among so many other quotes on so many different subjects.

79.   There are thousands of quotes from past Sages that support the teachings in the book you are now reading and that can be helpful or inspirational to spiritual aspirants. Future volumes of this book may have such quotes.   Information about where such quotes can be read online can be found at this website: www.seeseer.com

80.   All of the "spiritual" teachings of the past have been distorted and contaminated by the ego; therefore volume one, the book you are reading now, has very few quotes.

81.   Another reason the author did not previously realize the true meaning of I AM is that he had read that the "I AM," the true Self, is infinite continuous awareness.

82.   That made it seem like the "I AM" must be something different from the awareness that appears to wake up in the morning.

83.   However, the habit of always looking outward is what causes the awareness to appear to wake up in the morning and to seem limited.  The awareness does not really wake up in the morning and it is not limited. Waking up, going to sleep and limitation are illusions created by the habit of always looking outward.

84.    If one observes the awareness for many years, eventually one discovers that the awareness is continuous and that it is not limited.

85.    The significance of the Awareness Watching Awareness discovery is one of communication.

86.    A human could be told to focus on the I AM and even after one hundred million imaginary lifetimes, still not know what the I AM is.

87.    However, if told that the I AM is the awareness that appears to wake up in the morning, the background of awareness that is there during all the waking hours, and given specific instructions in how to turn the attention away from thought, etc., and towards awareness watching awareness, one can end the ego and suffering in this lifetime and remain eternally in bliss.

88.    Those specific practice instructions are in Chapter Seven.

89.    You might think that the majority of humans would rejoice at the discovery of the most direct and rapid means to eternal bliss.

90.    Due to the tricks of the ego, the majority of humans will not rejoice at the discovery.

91.    That is why this book begins by identifying the imposter, exposing its motivations and tricks, showing the importance of awakening the extremely intense desire for Liberation, and giving step-by-step instructions for such an awakening.

92.   Historically, not even one in a million humans has been dedicated to the direct experience of the eternal Truth that lives within them and is their true Self.

93.   The Awareness Watching Awareness Method is the most direct and rapid means for a human to end suffering and to remain in infinite-eternal-awareness-love-bliss.

94.   The Awareness Watching Awareness Method is the most direct and rapid means for a person of the Jewish faith to directly experience the "I AM" that was revealed to Moses.

95.   The Awareness Watching Awareness Method is the most direct and rapid means for a Christian to discover and live in the Kingdom of Heaven within in direct experience in this lifetime.

96.   The Awareness Watching Awareness Method is the most direct and rapid means for a "Hindu" to attain Liberation while living (jivanmukti) and to live in Being-Awareness-Bliss (sat-chit-ananda).

97.   The Awareness Watching Awareness Method is the most direct and rapid means for a Muslim to know the true Self.  The Prophet Mohammad said, "He who knows his Self knows his Lord."

98.   The Awareness Watching Awareness Method is the most direct and rapid means for a Buddhist to attain the bliss of Nirvana and to bring the ego, suffering, desire and craving to their final end.

99.   The ego has distorted all of the religious and spiritual teachings of the past.

The result is that all of the religious and spiritual teachings of the past now serve the ego and hide the most direct and rapid means to Liberation.

100.  What has happened with all of the religious and spiritual teachings of the past is that the ego in the reader or listener cooperates with the ego in the so-called "spiritual teacher" to produce a teaching that will serve the ego.  Then both the "spiritual teacher" and the student call the false teaching "a true teaching."

The "spiritual teacher" has different names in different spiritual traditions.  Some examples of this are: preacher, priest, minister, rabbi, master, guru, roshi, lama, imam, murshid, translator, etc.

The spiritual and religious teachings of the past are lineages of egotism that are falsely labeled and promoted as lineages of truth.

101.  Some of the spiritual teachings of the past were authentic spiritual teachings given by awakened sages.

102.  However, the moment an awakened sage speaks, the ego in the listener begins to distort the teachings.

103. Therefore, the distortion does not take time to begin.  The distortion begins immediately.

104.  Once the teaching has been distorted by the ego, the teaching serves the ego.

105.  The ego distortion becomes even greater as time passes.  The ego distortion can always be seen in both the written and spoken words of the spiritual and religious teachings of the past.

106. It is possible to extract helpful quotes from the spiritual teachings of the past; however, the quotes must be extracted by an awakened sage.

107. If an attempt to extract quotes is made by one in whom the extremely intense desire for liberation has not yet been awakened, some or all of the quotes selected will serve the ego.

108. Because it is the most direct and rapid means to end human misery and to live eternally in Peace-joy, the Awareness Watching Awareness Method is of great benefit even to those who are not spiritually inclined.

109. What might seem like only a slight difference in the way one practices makes a huge, profound, extraordinary, quantum leap of a difference in the speed of the results.

110. What might seem like only a slight difference in the way one practices can save years or even lifetimes of practice.

111. Therefore, the precision with which the practice instructions are described is crucial.

112. A slight change in the wording of the practice instructions will produce a slight change in the practice, thereby making the practice indirect, thus losing the rapid results.

113. There are other methods that appear similar to the Awareness Watching Awareness Method; however, seemingly similar methods will not produce the same rapid results and they will not save the years or lifetimes of practice.

114. Those other methods are different from the Awareness Watching Awareness Method and those differences destroy the efficiency.

115. In the Awareness Watching Awareness Method no external teacher is needed.

116. All that is required in the Awareness Watching Awareness Method is that one has the precise practice instructions and that one follows them by practicing.

117. At first the written instructions are the teacher; then the practice is the teacher.

118. The written instructions are the teacher only for the time it takes you to read them or listen to them, if you decide to record them.

119. Therefore, the teacher is the Awareness Watching Awareness practice. The Awareness Watching Awareness practice is the true, real, enduring teacher.

120. You never need to physically see a teacher on this Direct Path.

121. Physically seeing a teacher would draw your attention outward and would be counterproductive.

122. Instructions for practicing the Awareness Watching Awareness Method are in Chapter Seven.

123. The only way to find out if the Awareness Watching Awareness Method is or is not effective for you is to practice it.

124. If without trying it, you come to the conclusion that it will not be effective, then you have allowed the imposter (thinking) to rob you of a great opportunity.

125. With thinking you have a conclusion, an opinion or an assumption that may or may not be correct.

126. With practice you will know for sure whether the Awareness Watching Awareness Method is or is not effective for you.

127. Therefore, consider giving it a sincere, fair try.

128. A few months is not long enough to be a sincere, fair try.

Read Chapter Six very slowly three times before reading Chapter Seven.

# CHAPTER SEVEN

# THE

# AWARENESS WATCHING AWARENESS

# METHOD

# PRACTICE INSTRUCTIONS

## PRELIMINARY INSTRUCTIONS (1-73)

1.    Set aside as much time every day to practice the Awareness Watching Awareness Method as you are willing to set aside.

2.    Every day drop as many unnecessary activities as you can to create more time to practice the Awareness Watching Awareness Method.

3.    If you are not willing to drop all unnecessary activities, in order to create the maximum amount of time every day for practice, then you can read Chapter Five and Chapter Thirteen every day until the extremely intense desire for Liberation awakens in you.

4.    Eating food and taking a shower are examples of necessary activities.

5.    For some people working to earn a living is an example of a necessary activity.

6.    For some people taking care of their children is an example of a necessary activity.

7.    Some categories of unnecessary activities are entertainment, hobbies, etc.

8.     Practice for at least two hours every day.  Use all of your free time for practice, and practice for the maximum number of hours per day you are able to.

9.     If you are retired and can practice for twelve hours every day, consider doing so.

10.     It is better if you can be undisturbed and alone during your practice.

11.     If you practice at home, you can ask the people you live with not to disturb you when you are practicing unless there is an emergency.

12.     Or you can find some other place to practice where you will not be disturbed.  A quiet place is best.

13.     Bodily posture is not important in the Awareness Watching Awareness Method.

14.     However, since one wishes to turn the attention away from the body, it is important that the body is comfortable and relaxed and not causing any pain.

15.     You can do the practice sitting crossed legged, or sitting on a chair, or sitting on a sofa or couch, or even lying down on your bed if you are able to do so without falling asleep.

16.     Make sure the posture is comfortable and does not cause any pain or strain.

17.     Make sure the posture helps you to ignore the body and turn your attention away from the body. Make sure the posture does not cause your attention to be directed towards the body.

18.   For the purposes of this practice, the following definitions of the words awareness and thought must be used (19-46):

19.   Thought (19-21):   Thoughts are the words of your native language in your mind.

20.   If your native language is English, thoughts are those English words in your mind.

21.   If you are fluent in two languages, then thoughts are the words of those two languages in your mind.

22.   Awareness (22-46):   When you wake up from sleep, awareness is that consciousness that woke up from sleep.

23.   Thoughts come and thoughts go.   The background of awareness does not come and go.   The background of awareness is continuous during all your waking hours until you go to sleep again.

24.   Awareness is you, your consciousness, just your awareness that is looking through your eyes right now.

25.   The words awareness, consciousness, attention, observing, watching, looking, seeing and concentrating all have the same meaning in the practice instructions.

26.   Awareness is not thought.

27.   Awareness is that which is conscious of thought or conscious of the absence of thought.

28.   Both when there are thoughts and when there are no thoughts the background of awareness is aware.

The background of awareness is continuous during all of the waking hours until you go to sleep again.
During deep sleep, the thinker is no longer aware of the background of awareness.

29.   Awareness is not emotions.

30.   Awareness is that which is conscious of emotions or conscious of the absence of emotions.

31.   Both when there are emotions and when there are no emotions, the background of awareness is aware, because your awareness is continuous during all of the waking hours until you go to sleep again.

32.   Awareness is not the objects seen by the eyes.

33.   Awareness is that which is conscious of the objects seen by the eyes or conscious of the absence of the objects seen by the eyes.

34.   Your awareness is aware when the eyes are open seeing objects and when your eyes are closed not seeing objects, because your awareness is continuous during all the waking hours until you go to sleep again.

35.   Awareness is not the thought "I."

36.   Awareness is that which is conscious of the thought "I" or conscious of the absence of the thought "I."

37.   Both when you think "I" and when you do not think "I," your awareness is aware, because your awareness is continuous during all the waking hours.

38.   Awareness is not desire.

39.   Awareness is that which is conscious of desire or conscious of the absence of desire.

40.   Both when there is desire and when there is no desire, you are aware, because your awareness is continuous until you go to sleep again.

41.   Awareness is not something far away or mysterious.

42.   Awareness is that which is looking through your eyes reading this sentence.

43.   Just your ordinary, everyday awareness.

44.   Not some special awareness.

45.   Awareness is that which wakes up in the morning and remains conscious until you go to sleep at night.

46.   Awareness is not any of the things or experiences perceived.  Awareness is that which is conscious of the things or experiences.  Awareness is also that which is conscious of the absence of things or experiences.

47.   Try an experiment (48-52):

48.   Look at an object in the room.

49.   Notice the awareness looking through your eyes.

50.   Now shut your eyes and notice that you are still aware.

51.   It is the same awareness that a moment ago was looking at the room.

52.   Now, with your eyes still closed, observe your awareness.

53.   The following practice instructions (74-99 or A-Z) are the Awareness Watching Awareness Method described with carefully chosen slightly different words.

54.   The practice instructions are called Descriptions.

55.   Use only one Description per practice session.

56.   If you are going to practice for one, two or three hours today, then for that entire time, you should use the same Description.

57.   Try Description A first.

58.   Use a different description each day until you have tried all of the Descriptions.

59.   Then choose the Description that was the easiest for you to understand and to practice, and from then on use only that Description.

60.   Some Descriptions might for a moment have you start with your eyes open, however, once you are instructed to close your eyes, keep your eyes closed.

61.   The Awareness Watching Awareness Method is always practiced with the eyes closed.

62.   When you are observing your awareness, just remain with that.

63.   There is no need to do anything else.

64.   Awareness is empty.

65.    It is just awareness being aware of itself.

66.    It is not a special type of awareness.

67.    It is just your ordinary everyday awareness that you normally go through the day with, looking at itself.

68.    You can record the Descriptions on an audiocassette or CD, etc., for your personal use.

69.    Record only one Description per recording.

70.    Listen to only one Description during a practice session.

71.    It is better not to interrupt your practice session by having to turn your recording off.

72.    That is why it is best to record only one Description per recording.

73.    Repeat the same Description on the recording every thirty minutes.

# THE

# AWARENESS WATCHING AWARENESS

# METHOD

# PRACTICE INSTRUCTIONS

## (74-99 or A-Z):

74. Description A: Shut your eyes. Notice your awareness. Observe your awareness. Turn your attention away from the world, body and thought and towards awareness watching awareness. Every time you notice you are thinking, turn your attention away from thought and back towards awareness watching awareness. Watch your awareness, not your thoughts.

75. Description B: Look out at the room and notice your awareness looking out through your eyes. Now shut your eyes and notice the same awareness is still there that a moment ago was looking outward at the room. Observe that awareness. If you notice thoughts, ignore the thoughts and turn your attention away from the thoughts and towards awareness observing awareness.

76. Description C: Shut your eyes. Notice that you are conscious. Watch that consciousness. Every time you notice a thought, turn your attention away from the thought and continue watching your consciousness. Do not watch your thoughts. Watch your consciousness. Consciousness watching consciousness. Consciousness conscious of consciousness.

77. Description D: Shut your eyes. Turn your attention away from thought and watch the watcher.

78.   Description E:   Shut your eyes.   Notice your awareness. Be aware of your awareness. If you notice you are thinking, turn your attention away from thought and towards awareness of awareness.

79.   Description F:   Shut your eyes.   Just remain in awareness aware of itself.  If there are thoughts, turn your attention away from the thoughts and back to awareness aware of itself.

80.   Description G:   Shut your eyes.   You observe your awareness.   Whenever there are thoughts, turn your observation away from the thoughts and continue to observe your awareness.

81.   Description H:   Shut your eyes.   Turn your attention towards awareness and concentrate on awareness.  Concentrate in a relaxed manner without effort.   Every time thoughts are noticed, turn your attention away from the thoughts and back towards concentrating on awareness.

82.   Description I:   Shut your eyes.   Be aware of being aware.   Now remain in that awareness of awareness. If there are thoughts, turn your awareness away from the thoughts and continue being aware of being aware.

83.   Description J:   Shut your eyes.   Notice you are aware.  Look at that awareness.  Remain in awareness looking at awareness.   If thoughts arise, look away from the thoughts and continue looking at awareness. Remain in that awareness looking at awareness.

84.   Description K:   Shut your eyes.   Your present awareness watching your present awareness, while ignoring all else.

85. Description L: Look at the room. Notice your attention looking through your eyes. Shut your eyes and turn your attention around to look at itself. Attention attending to attention. Remain with that. Don't move from that. Don't attend to anything else. Don't attend to thought. Attend only to attention.

86. Description M: Look at the room. Notice your awareness looking through your eyes. Now shut your eyes. Notice that same awareness that was looking through your eyes a moment ago. Now turn that awareness around 180 degrees away from the world, the body and thought and towards itself, towards awareness aware of awareness.

87. Description N: Look at the room, or if you are outdoors look at the sky. Your awareness is the seer. Shut your eyes. See the seer. Turn your attention away from thought and towards the seer.

88. Description O: Shut your eyes. Turn your attention away from the known. Now know the knower.

89. Description P: Shut your eyes. Awareness aware only of awareness. Remain there. Dwell there. Be there. Live there.

90. Description Q: Shut your eyes. One awareness observing one awareness. Not two, one observing the other. Only one. Observe your awareness. If you notice thinking, do not attempt to complete the thought. Drop the thought, let go of the thought as though you had no interest in the thought. Continue observing your awareness.

91. Description R:  Shut your eyes.  Observe your awareness.  Relax into your awareness.  Remain there in awareness aware only of awareness.

92. Description S:  Shut your eyes.  Turn your awareness away from what your awareness is aware of and towards awareness aware only of itself.

93. Description T:  Shut your eyes.  Directly experience awareness by observing awareness and relaxing into awareness.  Rest in awareness of awareness.  Rest in awareness aware only of itself. Remain in awareness.  Do not remain in thought.

94. Description U:  There are the things you are aware of.  There is the awareness that is aware of the things.  Instead of observing the things, observe the awareness.  Shut your eyes.  There are thoughts and feelings.  There is the awareness that is aware of the thoughts and feelings.  Instead of observing the thoughts and feelings, observe the awareness.

95. Description V:  Shut your eyes.  Do not observe thought.  Observe awareness.  Awareness observing awareness is empty.  There is no thing to observe there.  Don't complicate it by thinking there is more to it.  Awareness is subtle.  In awareness observing awareness there is only awareness.  It is simple. Remain in awareness observing itself.

96. Description W:  Shut your eyes.  Focus on the awareness that thoughts are arising in.  Do not focus on the thoughts.  Thoughts come and thoughts go. The awareness in which thoughts are arising does not come and go.  Be aware of the awareness that does not come and go.  When there are thoughts, watch the awareness, not the thoughts.

When there are no thoughts, watch the awareness. Thoughts or no thoughts, continue to observe the awareness. Continue to relax in and be aware of awareness. Remain there. Dwell there. Be there. Live there.

97. Description X: Shut your eyes. If you see darkness, turn your attention away from the darkness and towards awareness of awareness. If you see light, turn your attention away from the light and towards awareness aware only of awareness. If you notice your breathing, turn your attention away from the breathing and towards awareness aware only of awareness. Whatever you become aware of, turn your attention away from it and towards awareness of awareness.

98. Description Y: Shut your eyes. Awareness not aware of thoughts. Awareness not aware of emotions. Awareness not aware of anything except awareness. Awareness aware of nothing except awareness. The background of awareness aware only of the background of awareness. Awareness aware only of awareness. Awareness only. Awareness alone.

99. Description Z: Shut your eyes. Let go of the idea that you own awareness. Let go of the idea that you control awareness. Let the infinite awareness be what it is without your trying to control it. Relax and observe the awareness. Let go of everything and observe the awareness. Relax completely and observe the awareness. With as little effort as possible and with a gentle, kind, easy, relaxed, loving approach; observe the awareness.

Read Chapter Seven three times very slowly before reading Chapter Eight.

# CHAPTER EIGHT

# FURTHER CLARIFICATION OF THE

# AWARENESS WATCHING AWARENESS

# METHOD

1.    These further clarifications have been placed in a separate chapter because the practice instructions for the Awareness Watching Awareness Method are simple and they should remain simple.

2.    It is not helpful to bring concepts with you into the practice.

3.    It is best just to focus on the simple practice instructions.

4.    One of the things you might wonder about is what to do after you start watching your awareness.

5.    There is nothing else to be done.

6.    You just continue with awareness watching awareness.

7.    There are no objects to see.

8.    Awareness is empty.    There is no thing to observe in awareness.

9.    Just continue for the entire practice session watching your awareness.    Only awareness watching awareness and nothing else.

10.    Don't expect any type of experience.

11.   If you wonder whether you will have some kind of spiritual experience, then that very wondering means you have added something to awareness watching awareness.

12.   Never add anything to awareness watching awareness.

13.   The key is to be content just watching your awareness and not to move from that and not to add anything to that.

14.   You may or may not have some kind of spiritual experience.   However, you should never expect any kind of spiritual experience.

15.   If you wonder if the state is going to deepen, that very wondering means you have added something to the Awareness Watching Awareness practice.

16.   Never add anything to the Awareness Watching Awareness Method.

17.   Just be content with awareness watching awareness.

18.   You should look at it like awareness watching awareness is all there is, there is nothing more.

19.   When practicing the Awareness Watching Awareness Method, you are not seeking anything.

20.   You are observing, not seeking.

21.   If you were seeking something, then there would be seeking and awareness watching awareness.

22.   That would mean you added seeking to the awareness watching awareness practice.

23.   Never add anything to the awareness watching awareness practice.   Just be content to continue with awareness watching awareness without adding anything to it.

24.   The best practice session is when there are no thoughts.

25.   If there are thoughts, turn your attention away from the thoughts and towards awareness watching awareness.

26.   Do not encourage thoughts.

27.   Do not try to complete a thought.

28.   Do not turn your attention towards thoughts.

29.   Do not think about thinking.

30.   If thoughts are happening, do not make a problem out of it.   Just turn your attention away from thoughts and towards awareness watching awareness.

31.   Just remain with awareness watching awareness.

32.   When awareness is watching awareness something extraordinary is happening.

33.   You are for the first time turning inward.

34.   Your true nature is awareness.

35.   What you really are at your core is awareness.

36.  Therefore, in awareness watching awareness, you are for the first time observing and knowing yourself.

37.  However, you should not think about that or anything else written in this chapter while practicing awareness watching awareness, because then you would be adding those thoughts to the practice.

38.  The reason for pointing out that you are doing something extraordinary while practicing awareness watching awareness is because at first you might think, "what else?" or "so what?"

39.  Just continue to practice and forget about "what else?" or "so what?"

40.  By turning your attention away from thought and towards awareness watching awareness, you are doing something that will change your life completely, if you are sincere and continue to practice.

41.  Most humans live their entire lives always looking outward at people, places and things.

42.  By turning your attention away from the world, body and thought and towards awareness watching awareness, you are doing something extraordinary.

43.  It might take a few days, a few weeks, or for some people a few months to start to feel something.

44.  At first it is subtle and you won't know what it is. You will know that you like it.

45.  It is pleasant.

46.  A new subtle feeling.

47.    You are beginning to feel eternal-life-love-peace.

48.    However, you should not have any expectations about that, because if you expect that, then you are adding that expectation to your awareness watching awareness practice.

49.    Never add anything to your awareness watching awareness practice.

50.    Just remain in awareness watching awareness while ignoring all else.

51.    Just stay there.

52.    Just remain in that.

53.    Don't look for something else.

54.    While you are practicing the Awareness Watching Awareness Method (55-89):

55.    Just stay there.

56.    Relax there.

57.    Don't seek something other than awareness watching awareness.

58.    Don't seek any other state.

59.    Don't seek deeper awareness.

60.    Don't seek anything.

61.    Just remain in awareness watching awareness.

62.  Be happy that it is simple.

63.  Don't seek more than that.

64.  It is just a simple state.

65.  Don't seek peace.

66.  Let peace come on its own, if it is going to come, without your expecting or seeking it.

67.  Just remain with awareness watching awareness, and every time a thought arises turn your awareness away from the thought and towards awareness watching awareness.

68.  Continue to practice every day.

69.  Look at it as though all you were seeking was the awareness watching awareness itself and not something else.  Be content with staying in awareness watching awareness without moving from it.

70.  Some days the mind may be noisy, however, if you keep on practicing, a good day will appear when your practice will go very deep without your trying to make it go deep.

71.  Never think about deep or shallow.

72.  If you think about deep or shallow, you would be adding something to the awareness watching awareness practice.

73.  Just be content to remain with awareness watching awareness, regardless if it seems like a good practice session or not.

74.　Some days your emotions may be turbulent.

75.　Ignore the turbulent feelings and turn your attention away from the emotions and towards awareness watching awareness.

76.　If you continue practicing the Awareness Watching Awareness Method every day, eventually you will start to enjoy awareness watching awareness.

77.　How long it will take to begin enjoying awareness watching awareness is different for different people.

78.　It may take days, weeks or for some people months before they begin to enjoy the practice.

79.　The point is, if you find it difficult to remain with awareness watching awareness in the beginning, don't give up.　Practice every day on the good days and on noisy-mind or turbulent-feeling days also.

80.　Just continue turning your attention away from thoughts and towards awareness watching awareness.

81.　You should not be expecting the day when you will start to enjoy awareness watching awareness, because then you would be adding something to the awareness watching awareness practice.

82.　The best kind of awareness watching awareness practice session is one that is empty.

83.　Awareness watching awareness and nothing else.

84.　Just stay there.

85.　Just be there.

86.     Dwell there.

87.     Remain there.

88.     Don't seek anything different; just be content with awareness watching awareness.

89.     Relax and continue watching your awareness.

90.     Here is a way to look at it (91-103):

91.     Awareness watching awareness is similar to falling in love.

92.     You spend time with someone.

93.     You watch them.  You observe them.

94.     You do not yet know them.

95.     You continue to observe them.

96.     You don't have expectations, because you don't know them well enough yet to have expectations.

97.     You continue to observe them.

98.     Some days you have pleasant feelings while you observe them.

99.     Some days you have unpleasant feelings while you observe them.

100.  You continue to observe them.

101. Every day you come to know them better, even though you may not be aware that you are coming to know them better.

102. Then one day, suddenly and unexpectedly, you fall in Love.

103. Awareness watching awareness is similar to that.

104. Just don't expect anything, and continue watching your awareness.

105. The fact that nothing is happening is great!

106. If it seems like day after day it is just the same, only awareness watching awareness; that is great!

107. Just remain content with that.

108. If you think it is going to change, then you are adding something to awareness watching awareness, in the form of an expectation that it is going to change.

109. Look at awareness watching awareness as enough, just as it is.

110. Continue your practice every day.

111. When will you fall in love with awareness watching awareness?

112. It may be after one month or after many months of practice.

113. There is plenty of confirmation along the way.

114. Do not be concerned about whether you are progressing or not. Progress may be imperceptible to the practitioner.

115. Some people will reach the point where just closing their eyes brings awareness-joy even before they have started the practice.

116. You should not expect it, because then you have added something to the Awareness Watching Awareness Method.

117. Some people may experience turbulence for many years before peace or vice versa.

118. Persevere and continue to practice.

119. You can look upon your awareness as something that wants you to watch it without expecting anything from it, like someone who wants to be loved for what they are and not for what they can give you.

120. Continue to watch awareness and do not expect peace-love-joy.

121. Let peace-love-joy come on its own, without your expecting it.

122. What you truly are is Infinite-Eternal-Awareness-Love-Bliss.

123. By having your attention turned towards the world, body and thought all the time, you imagine you are a body subject to disease, death and suffering.

124. By turning your attention towards awareness, you are for the first time observing what you are.

125. When practicing do not think about what you are.

126. Watch awareness without expecting anything.

127. Don't watch your thoughts.

128. Turn your attention away from your thoughts and watch your empty awareness.

129. Observe the observing.

130. Observe the awareness.

131. If you remain content with awareness watching awareness, your problems will start to disappear.

132. Your misery will start to disappear.

133. Peace will come unexpectedly.

134. Joy will come unexpectedly.

135. Infinite Love will come unexpectedly.

136. Awareness watching awareness is awareness being awareness.

137. Because of the long ancient habit of looking outward towards people, places and things, the word "watching" is used in some of the practice instructions.

138. One takes that same habit of watching people, places and things and shuts the eyes and turns it inwards towards awareness watching awareness.

139. That is why the word "watching" is used in some of the practice instructions.

140. What is real is awareness watching awareness, looking inward.

141. What is unreal is looking outward towards the world of people, places and things.

142. Looking outward brings suffering, death and futility.

143. Watching thoughts is not looking inward.

144. Watching feelings is not looking inward.

145. Watching breathing is not looking inward.

146. Only turning the attention away from the observed and towards the observer is looking inward.

147. Only awareness watching awareness is looking inward.

148. Looking inward is eternal liberation.

149. Looking inward is eternal life.

150. Looking inward is eternal awareness.

151. Looking inward is eternal peace.

152. Looking inward is eternal joy.

153. Looking inward is eternal Love that is absolutely perfect and free of all forms of sorrow and misery.

154. That joy, that perfection, is your awareness.

155. Because you always looked outward, you never experienced it.

156. To change the long habit of looking outward, you need to practice every day.

157. Practice for as many hours every day as you can.

158. If you only practice the Awareness Watching Awareness Method for thirty minutes per day and spend the other twenty-three and a half hours looking outward, you will not progress very quickly.

159. If you want rapid results, drop all your unnecessary activities to create the maximum amount of time to practice for many hours every day.

160. Maybe once per week, you can devote the whole day to practicing awareness watching awareness.

161. To come to know, experience, and live in Infinite-Eternal-Awareness-Love-Bliss is definitely worth the time spent practicing.

162. You'll discover you're not a body living in a world.

163. You are eternal awareness, perfect love-joy.

164. Don't expect any of the experiences described in this chapter, expectation will destroy the effectiveness.

165. If it seems boring the first few times you try the awareness watching awareness practice that is okay. Continue to practice.

Read Chapter Eight very slowly three times before reading Chapter Nine.

# CHAPTER NINE

# THE ABANDON RELEASE METHOD

1.    If your ego will not allow you to practice the Awareness Watching Awareness Method, the Abandon Release Method is the next best choice.

2.    The Awareness Watching Awareness Method is more effective than the Abandon Release Method.

3.    Therefore, if your ego will allow you to practice it, the Awareness Watching Awareness Method should be your first choice.

4.    If one looks at the thousands of spiritual practices that have been taught to humans in the past, the Awareness Watching Awareness Method is the most direct and rapid means to bring suffering and the ego to their final end in this lifetime.

5.    The Awareness Watching Awareness Method is the most direct and rapid means to living in infinite-eternal-awareness-love bliss in this lifetime.

6.    If one looks at the thousands of spiritual practices that have been taught to humans in the past, the Abandon Release Method is the second most rapid means to bring suffering and the ego to their final end in this lifetime.

7.    If one looks at the thousands of spiritual practices that have been taught to humans in the past, the Abandon Release Method is the second most rapid means to living in infinite-eternal-awareness-love-bliss in this lifetime.

8.    The Abandon Release Method is easier to practice than the Awareness Watching Awareness Method, even when you are tired or sleepy.

9.    If your ego will not allow you to practice the Awareness Watching Awareness Method, you could practice the Abandon Release Method for one year. Then you could switch to the Awareness Watching Awareness Method and practice it exclusively.

10.    Or you could continue practicing the Abandon Release Method for as many years as you wish.

11.    You should practice one or the other, the Awareness Watching Awareness Method or the Abandon Release Method, for the rest of your life.

12.    The reason practice should continue for as long as the body lives is (13-16):

13.    There is a false state of liberation, where the ego has not come to its final end, and has only been temporarily submerged in the infinite awareness.

14.    This temporary state is very similar to liberation, there is no suffering and one only has the experience of infinite awareness love bliss.

15.    One in this temporary state will usually have the perception that they have been liberated.

16.    However, one in this temporary state has not been liberated.  The ego will sooner or later reappear.
In True Liberation, the ego never reappears. In True Liberation, the ego is gone forever.

17. That (13-16) is the reason one should practice for as long as the body lives, even if one has the perception that one has been liberated.

18. The preliminary instructions for the Abandon Release Method are the same as for the Awareness Watching Awareness Method.

19. See Chapter Seven for the preliminary instructions.

20. In the beginning, the best position for the practice of the Abandon Release Method is lying down on your bed.

21. After you have practiced the Abandon Release Method many times while lying down, then you could try the practice sitting up.

22. After you have practiced the Abandon Release Method many times in both positions, sitting up and lying down, you can choose the position you like best and then continue to practice in that position.

23. The following is a suggested schedule for using the Abandon Release Method Descriptions:

24. Start by using the Description D practice instructions for the first month.

25. In other words, use Description D for thirty days.

26. Use Description E for the second month.

27. Continue using Description E for thirty days.

28. Use Description A for the third month.

29.    Continue using Description A for thirty days.

30.    Use Description B for the fourth month.

31.    Continue using Description B for thirty days.

32.    Use Description A (again) for the fifth month.

33.    Continue using Description A for thirty days.

34.    Begin using Description C.

35.    Continue to use Description C for one to four years.

36.    Once per month, as a reminder, for one practice session, use Description A.

37.    In other words, use Description C every day, and one day per month switch to Description A.

38.    After one to four years of practice you may be so familiar with the practice, Description F is all you need.

39.    If after one to four years of practice you switch to Description F, once per month for one practice session you should use Description C, and once per year for one practice session you should use Description A.

40.    Like any skill, the more you practice, the more skill you gain.

41.    The longer you practice, the more enjoyable the practice becomes, after you have gained some skill in letting go.

42. Some people will enjoy the Abandon Release Method from the beginning.

43. Other people will find the practice easy and enjoyable after many weeks of practicing every day.

44. You can make a recording of the practice instructions (Descriptions A, B, C, D, E or F) on an audio cassette or CD, for your personal use, and then play it during your practice session, repeating the instructions on the recording every thirty minutes. Pause for one minute between each sentence when making the recording.

45. Put the "do not disturb" sign on your bedroom door, turn off the lights, and lie down on your bed.

46. If lying down flat on your back becomes tiresome you can change positions by turning over on your side.

# THE ABANDON RELEASE METHOD

## PRACTICE INSTRUCTIONS

47.    Description A:  Shut your eyes.  Relax your body. Now ignore your body. Let go of all effort.  Let go of all sense of having to do something, as though there is nothing you have to do and nothing you have to think about.   Letting go of all effort means letting go of all will and all desire, as though there is nothing that needs to be accomplished or changed.  Let go.  Relax. Let go more.  Relax more.  See how far it is possible to let go.  Let go of all thoughts.  Let go of all feelings. Let go of all effort.  Let go of everything except your awareness.   Whatever thoughts, perceptions, images or feelings arise let them go as soon as they arise or even before they arise.   Do not follow thoughts, as though you had no interest in thoughts.  Let go of all your perceptions as if your perceptions have nothing to do with you.  Continue to relax more and more.

Throughout the practice session let go more, then let go even more and as the practice session continues, see how far it is possible to let go.  Relax completely. Let go totally.    Release everything except your awareness. Letting go is giving up completely. Letting go is surrendering completely.  Letting go is relaxing completely. Letting go is releasing completely. Letting go is letting go of all effort and all thought.  Letting go is letting go of all feelings, desires and images. Letting go is letting go of everything except your awareness. The difference between falling asleep and the Abandon Release Method is that when you fall asleep you let go of everything including your awareness.   In the Abandon Release Method you let go of everything except your awareness.

48.   Description B:  Shut your eyes.  Relax your body. Release your body.  Relax all effort.  Release all effort. Relax all your thoughts.  Release all your thoughts. Continue throughout the practice session to see how much you can relax and release your thoughts, feelings and desires.  Relax and release everything except your awareness.  Relax totally.  Relax completely.  Release totally.  Release completely.

49.   Description C:  Shut your eyes.  Let go of all effort.  Let go of all thought.  Let go of everything except your awareness.  Whatever arises let it go. Relax, release, let go.  Continue to relax, release and let go completely.  See how far it is possible to let go of all effort and all thought.  See how far it is possible to let go of everything except your awareness.

50.   Description D:  Shut your eyes.  Let go of all effort.  Continue to let go of all effort during the entire practice session.  Let go of effort more and more and see how far it is possible to let go of effort.  Relax and continue to relax.  Relax more and more throughout the entire practice session.  Totally let go of all effort.

51.   Description E:  Shut your eyes.  Let go of all thoughts.  If a thought arises, let it go.  If another thought arises, let it go.  Continue to let go of thought. Relax thought completely.  Continue to release thought throughout the practice session.  See how far it is possible to let go of thought.  Let go completely.

52.   Description F:  Shut your eyes.  Let go completely.  Totally let go.  Let go of everything except your awareness.

Read Chapter Nine very slowly three times before reading Chapter Ten.

# CHAPTER TEN

## THE ETERNAL METHOD

1.     The purpose of the Eternal Method is to provide a sense of the limitless nature of eternal life and to focus the attention on the eternal.

2.     Any position is okay for this practice.

3.     Lying down on your bed with the lights turned off is the best position.

4.     You may record the instructions for your personal use.    Pause for one minute between each sentence when making the recording.

5.     The Eternal Method is a secondary practice, not a primary practice; therefore, the Eternal Method should not be practiced more often than once per month.

## THE ETERNAL METHOD
## PRACTICE INSTRUCTIONS

6.     Shut your eyes.

7.     Imagine you are traveling back in time.

8.     Go back in time one hundred billion years.

9.     Go back in time one hundred billion more years.

10.    You are now so far back in time the earth does not exist.

11.    Imagine you are traveling back in time one trillion years further into the past.

12.   Go back in time one trillion more years.

13.   Imagine you are traveling back in time eight hundred trillion years further into the past.

14.   Now travel back eight hundred trillion years further into the past.

15.   Imagine that you are traveling at the rate of eight hundred trillion years per second into the past and that you have now traveled for one hundred trillion years at that rate.

16.   The contents of what was called universe at the time you lived on earth, do not yet exist at this time.

17.   None of the stars or planets that existed at the time you lived on earth exists yet, because you are now in a time before they existed.

18.   Travel eight hundred trillion years further back in time.

19.   Realize now that no matter how long you continue to travel back in time, you will not come any closer to the eternal past, because the eternal past goes on forever.

20.   Now travel another eight hundred trillion years further into the past.

21.   Now imagine you have traveled another eight hundred trillion years further into the past.

22.   Now travel another eight hundred trillion years further into the past.

23.    Realize that no matter how long you continue to travel into the past, even if you travel at the rate of eight hundred trillion years per second for a hundred trillion years, you will not come closer to the eternal past, because the eternal past always was, forever.

24.    Look into the eternal past and see: *always was*.

25.    The objects in space come and go; however, the space is eternal.

26.    Realize the meaning of *the eternal past*.

27.    See: *the eternal past goes on forever and ever*.

28.    Look into the eternal past, which goes on forever and ever, and see the meaning of *always was*.

29.    Look into the eternal past and see the meaning of *the eternal past has no beginning*.

30.    Look into the eternal past and see the meaning of *no end*.

31.    Realize: *the eternal past has no end*.

32.    Look into the eternal past and see: *the eternal past goes on forever and never ends*.

33.    Now come back to the present time.

34.    Imagine you are traveling forward in time.

35.    Travel one hundred billion years into the future.

36.    Now travel one hundred billion years further into the future.

37.   You are now so far into the future the earth and sun no longer exist.

38.   Travel one trillion years further into the future.

39.   Now imagine that you have traveled one trillion more years into the future.

40.   Now travel eight hundred trillion years further into the future.

41.   Now imagine that you have traveled another eight hundred trillion years further into the future.

42.   Imagine that you are traveling at the rate of eight hundred trillion years per second into the future and that you have traveled for one hundred trillion years at that rate.

43.   You are now in a time when everything that existed during the time when you lived on earth, no longer exists.

44.   All of the stars and planets that existed at the time when you lived on earth, no longer exist.

45.   All of the things that you thought were so important when you lived on earth, have no importance now.

46.   Look at how all of the problems you thought you had when living on earth, have no significance now.

47.   Look at how all those problems you had when you lived on earth did not have any real significance. You only imagined those problems had significance.

48. What has real value and significance is the eternal.

49. The eternal infinite space-awareness, which is eternal life, is what you are and what you always have been, and that is where all real significance, Truth, meaning, perfect safety, love and bliss are.

50. Now imagine you have traveled another eight hundred trillion years further into the future.

51. Now travel another eight hundred trillion years into the future.

52. Realize now that no matter how long you continue to travel into the future, you will not come any closer to the eternal future, because the eternal future goes on forever.

53. Now travel another eight hundred trillion years further into the future.

54. Now imagine you have traveled another eight hundred trillion years further into the future.

55. Realize, no matter how long you continue to travel into the future, even if you travel at the rate of eight hundred trillion years per second for one hundred trillion years, you will not come closer to the eternal future, because the eternal future continues forever.

56. Now look into the eternal future and see the meaning of *always will be*.

57. The objects in space come and go; however, the space is eternal.

58.    Realize the meaning of *the eternal future*.

59.    See the meaning of *the eternal future goes on and on forever*.

60.    See the eternal future that goes on forever and ever and realize the meaning of *always will be*.

61.    Look into the eternal future and see the meaning of *no end*.

62.    See: *the eternal future has no end*.

63.    See the eternal future and see the meaning of *the eternal future goes on forever and never ends*.

64.    You are that eternal infinite space-awareness that never ends.

65.    See the beauty of eternal life.

66.    Come back to the present time and dedicate every moment of your life to the realization of the Direct Experience of who you really are at your core.

67.    In your daily life don't let the imposter; who is the mistaken identity called ego, take you through distractions, detours and activities that lead to the temporary, because the temporary is meaningless, futile, and leads to suffering.

68.    Drop all distractions, detours, entertainment and other useless activities to create the maximum amount of time for the practice of the most direct and rapid means to eternal bliss.

69.    Never waste time.

70.   Never waste even one second.

71.   Discover your Eternal Life in Direct Experience.

72.   See who you really are at the core of your being.

73.   See who you are at the core of your awareness.

74.   The core of your awareness is infinite and eternal.

75.   A wave on an ocean of consciousness imagines there is a line separating it from the ocean.

76.   One day the wave challenges that assumption by diving deep down.

77.   The wave discovers there is no line separating it from the ocean.

78.   The wave discovers there are no waves; there is only the ocean.

79.   You are infinite-eternal-awareness-love-bliss.

80.   Realize who you are in Direct Experience.

81.   Bring the imposter self to an end.

82.   Discover your true Self in Direct Experience.

Read Chapter Ten very slowly three times before reading Chapter Eleven.

## CHAPTER ELEVEN

## THE INFINITE SPACE METHOD

1.    When people practice the Awareness Watching Awareness Method, they often tend to have the perception that awareness is located in their head.

2.    Your awareness is not in your head.

3.    Your awareness is infinite.

4.    The Infinite Space Method helps to remove the perception that awareness is something in your head.

5.    The Infinite Space Method helps to provide a sense of the limitless nature of space.

6.    The Infinite Space Method is a secondary, not a primary method; therefore, the Infinite Space Method should not be practiced more often than once per month.

7.    You can practice the Infinite Space Method in any position; however, for the first time, try practicing lying down on your bed with the lights turned off.

8.    You may record the instructions for your personal use.   Pause for one minute between each sentence when making the recording.

# THE INFINITE SPACE METHOD

## PRACTICE INSTRUCTIONS

### (9-84)

9.    Shut your eyes.

10.    Imagine you are traveling into outer space, in one direction, in a straight line.

11.    Imagine you have traveled eight hundred trillion miles into outer space.

12.    Continue in the same direction, along the same line, and travel another eight hundred trillion miles further into outer space.

13.    Now imagine you have traveled another eight hundred trillion miles further into space.

14.    Now imagine you have traveled another eight hundred trillion miles further in the same direction.

15.    Now imagine that you are traveling at the speed of one hundred thousand miles per second, and that you have traveled for eight hundred trillion years at that speed, in the same direction, along the same line.

16.    Now travel for another eight hundred trillion years, in the same direction, at the rate of one hundred thousand miles per second.

17.   No matter how fast you travel, and no matter how long you travel, you have not come any closer to infinite space, because infinite space never ends.

18.   Now travel another eight hundred trillion miles, in the same direction, along the same line.

19.   Now imagine you have traveled another eight hundred trillion miles in the same direction.

20.   Now travel another eight hundred trillion miles in the same direction, along the same line.

21.   Now look forward in the same direction and see: *infinite space never ends*.

22.   Now look forward in the same direction and see: *space never ends*.

23.   Now travel another eight hundred trillion miles further in the same direction, along the same line.

24.   Now imagine you have traveled another eight hundred trillion miles further in the same direction.

25.   Now look forward in the same direction and see: *space goes on forever and ever*.

26.   See that even if you travel in the same direction for all eternity, you will never come to the end, because space never ends.

27.   Look in the same direction and see infinite space.

28.   Look in the same direction and see: *space goes on forever and there is no end*.

29. Realize: *space is never ending in all directions.*

30. That infinite space is your awareness.

31. That infinite space is infinite love.

32. That infinite space is eternal life.

33. See the infinite freedom of infinite space.

34. See: *infinite space is open to allow everything.*

35. Whatever wall or boundary you imagine; there is infinite space on the other side of that boundary.

36. If you imagine a circle, there is always a larger circle, and there is always infinite space on the outside of the circle.

37. Now come back to earth.

38. Imagine you are sitting outdoors on a chair.

39. There is space in the atoms of your body.

40. There is space between the atoms of your body.

41. There is space in the molecules of your body.

42. Space is between the molecules of your body.

43. There is space in the cells of your body.

44. There is space between the cells of your body.

45. Your body is space.

46.  Space in and between the atoms, molecules and cells of your body is touching the space in the atmosphere.

47.  Space in the atmosphere is touching outer space.

48.  The imagined boundaries are also space.

49.  The earth, and everything on the earth, is space.

50.  All the planets and stars in the universe are space.

51.  There is only one space.

52.  Space is the source of life.

53.  Space is alive.

54.  One infinite space.

55.  One infinite Love.

56.  You are that infinite Love.

57.  One eternal-infinite-space-awareness-love-bliss.

58.  You are that one eternal-infinite-space-awareness-love-bliss.

59.  There is only that one eternal-infinite-space-awareness-love-bliss.

60.  All the boundaries are imagined.

61.  There are no real boundaries.

62. In Reality there is only the infinite freedom of infinite space.

63. From time to time in your daily life, focus on the space, instead of on the objects.

64. Space inside the objects, space outside the objects, and space in the imagined boundary.

65. Never again imagine that space is just nothing.

66. Space is that which is truly valuable.

67. Space is eternal life-awareness.

68. Space is infinite Love.

69. One being, one space, one infinite Love.

70. Space projecting space into space.

71. Focusing attention on space is focusing attention on infinite freedom.

72. Focusing attention on space is focusing attention on infinite Love.

73. Your awareness is space.

74. All limits are imagined.

75. All limits are a product of delusion.

76. All limits are a type of dream.

77. It is possible to wake up.

120

78.   You can wake up to the Reality of infinite-eternal-space-awareness-love-bliss.

79.   You can wake up to perfect peace.

80.   You can wake up and discover you have always been eternal-life-love-awareness-joy.

81.   You can wake up and discover you will always be eternal-life-love-awareness-joy.

82.   Because of the long habit of imagining you are a thinker living in a body in a world, waking up requires spending much time in the direct spiritual practice.

83.   You are not a thinker living in a body in a world.

84.   You are infinite-eternal-space-awareness-love-joy.

Read Chapter Eleven very slowly three times before reading Chapter Twelve.

# CHAPTER TWELVE

## THE LOVING ALL METHOD

1.   All of the methods that have been described in previous chapters are to be practiced when one is not engaged in any other activities.

2.   The question may arise, "What is the most effective method that can be practiced while one is engaged in other activities?"

3.   The Loving All Method is the most effective method that can be practiced while one is engaged in other activities.

4.   The Loving All Method can be practiced everyday, during any and all types of activities.

# PRACTICE INSTRUCTIONS

## FOR THE LOVING ALL METHOD
### (5-32)

5.    The Loving All Method can be summed up as follows:  Love everything you perceive, exactly as it is. Love everything you experience, exactly the way it is.

6.    Love every thought you have, exactly as it is.

7.    Love those thoughts you think are good, exactly the way they are.

8.    Love those thoughts you think are bad, exactly the way they are.

9.    Love all your emotions, exactly the way they are.

10.   If you feel happy, love your happiness, exactly the way it is.

11.   If you feel sad, love your sadness, exactly the way it is.

12.   If you feel courage, love your courage, exactly the way it is.

13.   If you feel fear, love your fear, exactly as it is.

14.   If you feel love, love your feeling of love, exactly the way it is.

15.   If you feel anger, love your feeling of anger, exactly the way it is.

16.   Love your body, exactly the way it is.

17.   Love the objects you see, exactly as they are.

18.   Love the people you see, just the way they are.

19.   Love your actions, just as they are.

20.   Love everything you feel, think, say or do, exactly the way it is.

21.   Love everything you see, taste, touch, smell or hear, exactly the way it is.

22.   Love everything other people do, feel, think or say, exactly the way it is.

23.   If someone says something nice to you, love what the person says, exactly the way it is.

24.   If someone says something mean to you, love what the person says, exactly the way it is.

25.   If someone says to you, "You are the nicest person I have ever met," love what the person said, exactly the way they said it.

26.   If someone says to you, "You are the most disgusting person I have ever met," love what the person said, exactly the way they said it.

27.   If something nice happens during your day, love it exactly the way it is.

28.   If something horrible happens during your day, love it exactly the way it is.

29.   Love everything that happens, just the way it is.

30.   Love every activity, exactly the way it is.

31.   Love every experience, exactly the way it is.

32.   Love everything, exactly the way it is.

## FURTHER CLARIFICATION

## OF THE LOVING ALL METHOD

33.   If you don't understand how to practice using the word "love," you can substitute the words "emotionally allow" for the word "love" in the practice instructions.

34.   After practicing every day for one month using the words "emotionally allow," you can substitute the words "emotionally accept" for the word "love" in the practice instructions.

35.   After practicing every day for one month using the words "emotionally accept," you can go back to the original wording of the instructions, just as they are, using the word "love," and then continue using the word "love" from then on.

36.   The Loving All Method refers only to emotions.

37.   No changes in external behavior are required.

38.   For example, if a vase falls and you would normally try and catch it, you will also try and catch the vase while practicing the Loving All Method.

39. You do not allow the vase to fall because you love the falling. You can love the falling and you can also love the attempt at catching the vase.

40. If someone were to try to punch you in the face and you would normally duck, you will also duck while practicing the Loving All Method.

41. Loving the fact that someone is trying to punch you does not mean you will not duck.

42. You also love ducking to avoid being punched.

43. The Loving All Method is emotional acceptance.

44. The Loving All Method is not changing actions.

45. The Loving All Method is like any skill: the more you practice, the more skill you gain.

46. If someone says something mean to you and you feel bad emotionally because of what they said; love the negative emotion as it is, and love yourself.

47. In the beginning, even though you are attempting to love everything and every experience exactly as it is, you may or may not succeed in loving everything and every experience exactly as it is.

48. Changing the long time habit of emotionally rejecting experiences will require much practice.

49. Love as much as you can love.

50. Continue to practice every day, trying to love everything and every experience exactly the way it is.

51.   After you have practiced for a few months, you will gain more success at loving more experiences exactly the way they are.

52.   For some people, it may take years of practice to be able to love all experiences.   However, great benefits come right from the beginning, from the very first time you love an experience that you would have previously rejected.   There is more love and energy in your life; and life is lighter and easier.   Therefore, it is not as though you have to wait for some big payoff at the end of the Loving All Method.   Each day you gain more skill at loving your experiences, you have more love and energy on that very day.

53.   Every day, try to love everything and every experience that happens exactly the way it is.   The key word is try.   Try means do it.   You will learn how by trying.   You will learn how by doing it.   It might take some time to gain skill.   It might take some time to succeed.   Some people may have great success from the very first time they try.   Other people may have to practice for a few months to see great changes in the ability to love what previously seemed unlovable.

54.   Loving everything the way it is includes emotional acceptance.

55.   Emotional acceptance does not prevent you from trying to change whatever you wish to change.

56.   What you wish to change, you will still change.

57.   Whatever action you would normally take to change something, you will take that same action while practicing the Loving All Method.

58.   If you have a negative emotion while practicing the Loving All Method, you love the negative emotion. That may or may not change the negative emotion.

59.   Even if loving the negative emotion does not change the negative emotion, continue to love the negative emotion and the experiences that created the negative emotion exactly the way they are. Every day, continue to gain skill at loving negative emotions exactly as they are and eventually you may start to see some of the negative emotions change into love.

60.   You should not look inward while engaged in daily activities.

61.   You should look outward while engaged in daily activities.

62.   In other words, it is important to pay attention to what you are doing while engaged in daily activities.

63.   The Loving All Method is not *looking inward*.

64.   It is important to pay close attention during your daily activities to minimize errors and problems.

65.   If you try to look inward during your daily activities, your activities may not flow smoothly.

66.   For example, if you try to look inward while putting toothpaste on your toothbrush, you might put shampoo or shaving cream on your toothbrush because your attention is divided between outward and inward.

67.   Fortunately, the Loving All Method does not require inward attention.

68.   The Loving All Method does not require much thought either.   In the beginning you might need to think something like "Love every experience" many times every day while you are learning the practice.

69.   However, after much practice you will not need that thinking reminder.  The Loving All Method is a new feeling habit.   The practice is feeling, not thinking. Because the practice requires little or no thought and is not a *looking-inward* method, it can be practiced during all daily activities.

70.   The Loving All Method is a way to develop the habit of feeling love towards everything you perceive.

71.   In the beginning you could try practicing "no emotional resistance" during all of your daily activities.

72.   In action you can resist all you want to resist.

73.   If you would normally resist something in action, you will continue to resist it in action while practicing the Loving All Method.

74.   Not resisting emotionally has nothing to do with what you do in your actions, activities and behavior.

75.   You can continue to resist all you wish to resist in your actions, activities and behavior while practicing the Loving All Method.

76.   While you may be resisting in action, you do not resist emotionally while practicing the Loving All Method.

77.   Loving every experience exactly the way it is, makes living much easier.

78.    Loving every experience exactly the way it is, frees energy that used to be wasted.

79.    Loving every experience exactly the way it is, can change your daily living to a life of radiant love.

80.    Thus, the Loving All Method can fill your life with energy, ease, love, and joy.

Read Chapter Twelve very slowly three times before reading Chapter Thirteen.

# CHAPTER THIRTEEN

## THE REMINDERS

1.    Read Chapter Five and Chapter Thirteen every day until the extremely intense desire for Liberation awakens.

2.    You will know the extremely intense desire for Liberation has awakened when you have dropped all unnecessary activities to create the maximum amount of time for spiritual practice.

3.    If you do not do your spiritual practice every day, eventually your life will become full of suffering.

4.    If you do not do your spiritual practice every day, eventually, sooner or later, you will experience one or more of the thousands of different types of suffering.

5.    If you do not do your spiritual practice every day, you will continue to be caught in the cycle of birth and death, birth again, death again, birth again, death again, and in that cycle, eventually, you will experience all of the thousands of forms of suffering.

6.    If you do not do your spiritual practice every day, you will experience death, diseases, violence and thousands of types of suffering, lifetime after lifetime.

7.    If you do your spiritual practice every day for the maximum amount of time you can create by dropping all unnecessary activities, eventually all forms of suffering will end and you will live in Infinite-Eternal-Awareness-Love-Bliss.

8.    The purpose of spiritual practice is to experience infinite-eternal-awareness-love-bliss in this lifetime, not in the afterlife or some future lifetime.

9.    All delays are tricks of the ego.

10.    All detours are tricks of the imposter self.

11.    All distractions are tricks of the false pretend self.

12.    Every thought that leads you away from spiritual practice is a trick created by the imposter.

13.    Look at your daily activities and drop all those activities that are not necessary, to create as much time as possible for spiritual practice everyday.

14.    Bathing and eating food everyday are necessary.

15.    For most people working to earn a living everyday is necessary.

16.    Entertainment is not necessary.

17.    Make sure your spiritual practice is the most direct and rapid means to infinite-eternal-awareness-love-bliss.

18.    You have a choice between CHOICE A (19-21):

19.    Infinite-Eternal-Awareness-Love-Bliss    with    no suffering.

20.    Absolutely perfect Love-Bliss for all eternity.

21.    Living in and knowing your true Self, eternally.

22.   Or CHOICE B (23-26):

23.   Thousands of forms of suffering, sorrow, violence, diseases and death, over and over again, death-rebirth-death-rebirth-death-rebirth-death.

24.   Living from and knowing an imposter self.

25.   Living from an acquired false self (thought).

26.   Living from a parasite pretending to be your self.

27.   Make CHOICE A.

28.   Every day you do your spiritual practice, you are making CHOICE A.

29.   Every day you do not do your spiritual practice, you are making CHOICE B.

30.   Read Chapters Five and Thirteen every day.

31.   The pretend self is very tricky and tries to lead people away from spiritual practice.

32.   Reading Chapters Five and Thirteen every day will help combat the ego's tricks.

33.   Every day look at your activities and drop all activities that are not really necessary.

34.   Every day create as much time as possible for spiritual practice.

35.   Do your spiritual practice every day.

36.   Every day you have a CHOICE.

37. You cannot change yesterday's choices, therefore, do not worry about yesterday's choices.

38. What you can do is:

**Do your spiritual practice today.**

39. Before the extremely intense desire for Liberation is awakened, the false self will lead you to a practice that will support the ego.

40. After the extremely intense desire for Liberation is awakened, you will be lead to the spiritual practice that is the most rapid means to Infinite-Eternal-Awareness-Love-Bliss.

41. After the extremely intense desire for Liberation is awakened, you will be able to see how the ego has contaminated all of the spiritual and religious teachings of the past, including both esoteric and exoteric teachings.

42. Reading Chapter Five and Chapter Thirteen every day may be enough to awaken in you the extremely intense desire for Liberation.

43. Self-honesty is a great help towards awakening the extremely intense desire for Liberation.

44. Watch the ego when it tries to lead you away from spiritual practice into distractions, detours, diversions, delays, unnecessary activities and entertainment. **Do not let the ego win that battle.**

45. Time is precious. A human lifespan is very short. You have been shown the most direct and rapid means to eternal bliss in this lifetime.

Hundreds of millions of lifetimes may pass before you have this opportunity again. Value every second. Don't waste a second.

46. Do not waste time in activities that lead only to that which is temporary and therefore futile.

47. Ask of each activity, "Where can this lead?"

48. Ask of each activity, "Can this lead to eternal bliss, or does this lead to that which is temporary?"

49. There are thousands of quotes from the spiritual teachings of the past that support the teachings in the book you are now reading.

50. However, the time you spend in practice is a trillion times more beneficial than time spent reading.

51. Therefore, if you are willing to practice, practice.

52. If you are not willing to practice, even after reading Chapter Five and Chapter Thirteen hundreds of times, then you could try reading some quotes by other authors. For recommendations on where to read the most powerful spiritual teachings, see future volumes of this book or this website:

www.seeseer.com

53. Choose the Direct Experience of infinite-eternal-**existence-being-life**, here and now in this lifetime, by making it the first priority in your life, and by centering your entire life on your spiritual practice.

54.    Choose the Direct Experience of infinite-eternal-**awareness**, here and now in this lifetime, by making it the first priority in your life, and by centering your entire life on your spiritual practice.

55.    Choose the Direct Experience of infinite-eternal-**bliss**, here and now in this lifetime, by making it the first priority in your life, and by centering your entire life on your spiritual practice.

56.    Choose the Direct Experience of infinite-eternal-**love**, here and now in this lifetime, by making it the first priority in your life, and by centering your entire life on your spiritual practice.

57.    Once you have dropped all unnecessary activities and are using all of the free time thus created to practice the Awareness Watching Awareness Method, you do not need to continue to read this or any other spiritual book.  It would be better at that stage if you stopped reading all spiritual books including this one.

58.    If you find that at some point a substantial amount of your time has slipped back into unnecessary activities, then you could try reading Chapter Five and Chapter Thirteen every day until you have once again dropped all unnecessary activities, and are using all of the free time thus created to practice the most direct and rapid means to eternal bliss.

59.    If reading Chapter Five and Chapter Thirteen every day for a few months does not result in your dropping all unnecessary activities to free up the maximum amount of time for your spiritual practice, then you could read the entire book again, very slowly, starting with the introduction, then Chapter One, etc.

60. After you have dropped all unnecessary activities and are using all of the free time thus created for your spiritual practice, the teachings and the path are very simple. At that stage you should not try and remember any of the teachings from this book.

61. After you have reached the stage where you have dropped all unnecessary activities and are using all of the free time thus created to practice the Awareness Watching Awareness Method, you can simplify the teachings by focusing upon the following (62-65):

62. *Drop all unnecessary activities to create the maximum amount of time to practice the Awareness Watching Awareness Method.*

63. *It is best to practice in a place where you will be undisturbed. Set aside time exclusively for practice, with no other activities occurring.*

64. *Choose one of the practice descriptions and practice according to one of those descriptions.*

65. *For example, Description G: "Shut your eyes. You observe your awareness. If there are thoughts, turn your attention away from the thoughts and continue to observe your awareness."*

66. In the above example (62-65), there are eighty-four words to focus upon. Depending on which Awareness Watching Awareness Method practice description you choose, the number of words will be slightly different. Thus if you wish to keep the teachings simple, free of extra concepts, you can do so with very few words.

67.    The point is, this is really a very simple path and much of the book is for the purpose of helping you to reach the point where you drop all unnecessary activities to spend the maximum amount of time in practice.

68.    Once you have reached that point, eighty-four words, give or take a few words, can become your focus to make the teaching very simple.

69.    For those of you who have **not** reached the point where you have dropped all unnecessary activities to create the maximum amount of time to practice the most direct and rapid means to eternal bliss, **summarizing the book would be a huge mistake.**

70.    This book contains a unique step-by-step formula beginning from the Introduction, through Chapter 14.

71.    All of the steps, from a detailed description of the imposter, to understanding how the imposter arose, seeing the difference between the imposter and the true Self, understanding the imposter's tricks, the methods used to see that thought has no real foundation, the importance of awakening the extremely intense desire for liberation, the methods to awaken the extremely intense desire for liberation, the Awareness Watching Awareness Method, The Abandon Release Method, The Eternal Method, The Infinite Space Method, and The Loving All Method are essential for most people, due to the tricks of the ego.

72.    To use the eleven steps mentioned in 71 above to summarize the teachings in this book would once again be a huge mistake, because one would be leaving out so many essentials that make this book the unique and immensely valuable contribution that it is.

73.   What is new on a combination lock that you have been unable to open is not the numbers on the dial. What is new is the combination that opens the lock.

74.   What makes this book unique is the particular step-by-step formula or recipe described in 167 pages.

75.   Many of the ingredients have been mentioned in the spiritual teachings of the past.   They have been mixed with ever so many non-essentials.   Removing all the non-essentials and placing only the essentials into one book is one of the factors that make this book unique and something new under the sun.

76.   If you find some similar sentences in this book and some of the spiritual books of the past that in no way changes the fact that this book is quite different from all of the spiritual books written in the past.   One fragment in one book and another fragment in another book is not the precise formula that is most effective for liberation from the ego.

77.   For example, very few spiritual books give a detailed description of the difference between the ego and the true Self.   Of those that do, very few describe how the imposter arose.   Of those that do, very few go into detail describing the tricks the ego uses to preserve its imaginary self.   Of those that do, very few have listed the awakening of the extremely intense desire for Liberation as the solution to every problem a spiritual seeker encounters, including the trillions of tricks the ego can generate.   Of those that do, very few have given a step-by-step method of awakening the extremely intense desire for Liberation.   Of those that do, very few have pointed out that all of the "spiritual" teachings of the past have been contaminated by the ego and now serve the ego.

Of those that do, very few have described the Most Direct and Rapid Means to Eternal Bliss.

78.    There are more than fifteen hundred sentences in this book.   Those sentences describe a very precise formula.   If the formula is changed, the formula will usually no longer be effective.   Fragments of the formula have been stated in some of the teachings of the past.   The formula has never appeared in the spiritual teachings of the past.   No book ever written has contained the exact formula described in these 167 pages, while leaving out all of the non-essentials.

79.    Anyone claiming that the step-by-step formula taught in the fourteen chapters and more than fifteen hundred sentences of this book has been taught before is making a false statement.   Some of the ingredients in the recipe have been taught before; therefore not all of the ingredients are new.   What is new is this particular formula that includes only the essentials, and exposes the ego's tricks and the ego's effects.

80.    Awareness watching awareness, which can be described in many ways such as; *awareness aware only of awareness* was taught in a very small number of the spiritual teachings of the past.   It was ignored in those very same teachings, buried by the ego in thousands of non-essentials.   To remove all the non-essentials and restore awareness watching awareness to its rightful place as the most direct and rapid means to eternal bliss is new.   That is only one fragment of this formula.

81.    The repetition in this book is deliberate.   It is far more effective to have an insight into five points that permanently change one's consciousness, than to collect information about a thousand so-called "spiritual" teachings and remain as a sleeping egotist.

82.　Making a simple spiritual teaching into something complicated is a trick generated by the ego.

83.　Thus, communicating only the essentials in simple plain language is quite deliberate in this book.

84.　Similar words will usually not produce the same results. The new wording in this book, that leaves out the non-essentials and points directly to the essentials, can produce very different results.

85.　For those of you who realize the great unique value in this book, it would be an error to think that everyone will see it.

86.　Those who are spiritually immature or who lack intelligence, discernment, sincerity, discrimination or the ability to perceive subtle differences, will not see the unique and tremendous value of this book.

87.　The ego will prevent those who are spiritually immature from seeing what is revealed in this book. The ego will block from their view most of what is written in the more than fifteen hundred sentences in this book. They will then find some other excuse for why they do not see the unique value of what is here.

88.　This book is a new doorway for humanity.

89.　For the first time in human history a spiritual book has dealt with and exposed in detail the tricks of the ego; their extent, their cause and the solution, without any ego contamination or non-essentials.

90.　This book has created a spiritual revolution.
At the beginning, only a small number will see this.
In the years ahead, many will see this.

91.   What has been presented in this book is that which is most essential.  For those who think they need more, future volumes of this book or books listed on the websites mentioned in this book will have supplements.

92.   Reading the book at different times in your life can produce different results.

93.   If, even after reading this book many times, the ego did not allow you to see the value of what is here, try reading the book again a few months or a year from now or when your openness or desire for Freedom  has increased.

94.   For those of you who have reached the point where you have dropped all unnecessary activities to create the maximum amount of time to practice the most direct and rapid means to eternal bliss, if you choose to add something, the recommendation would be to add the Loving All Method.

95.   All of the methods in the book except the Loving All Method are to be practiced when there are no other activities going on.

96.   The Loving All Method can be practiced during all activities.  Thus the Loving All Method is a means to use all of your time productively towards your awakening.

97.   For thousands of years humans have passed a nightmare world full of suffering, lies, deceit, fear, anger, and violence unto their children.  To stop this cycle: challenge the assumptions, ideas, beliefs and concepts that were taught to you at a young age and now form the basis for your perceptions.

98. Although it was suggested that you suspend doubt long enough to see what is presented in this book, you need not suspend doubt forever.

99. Doubt is a very valuable tool in the process of awakening.

100. You could begin by doubting all of the religious and spiritual teachings of the past.

101. Then doubt every human belief in all fields including science and philosophy.

102. Then doubt the validity, sincerity and existence of the doubter. Find out: *who or what is the doubter*?

103. Then practice the most direct and rapid means to eternal bliss.

104. Then, eventually, sooner or later, experience the absolute perfection of Infinite-Eternal-Awareness-Love-Bliss. Then continue to practice.

105. For this to happen you have to begin to care.

106. Care about Truth enough to see that the human past has been a falsehood.

107. Care about Truth enough to drop the past ideas, beliefs, concepts and opinions. Then begin a new life.

108. The ego and its tricks is the lock. It is a combination lock. The combination to this lock is revealed for the first time in history in the more than fifteen hundred sentences in this book beginning with the Introduction and continuing through Chapter 14. On the other side of the door is eternal Life-Love-Bliss.

# CHAPTER FOURTEEN

# EXPERIENCES

# THE JOURNEY

# AND

# THE FINAL GOAL

1.     Many spiritual teachings have maps or lists of stages or signs of progress.

2.     All such maps or lists are false.

3.     There are no uniform signs or stages.

4.     One aspirant may have a very noisy mind two moments before the ego's final end, then one moment of silence, then the ego's final end.

5.     Another aspirant may have a long extended period of silence before the ego's final end.

6.     One way to understand this is to take the example of a dream or of sleep.

7.     What are the signs or indications that you are waking up from a dream or from sleep?

8.     There may be such signs, but they differ not only from person to person but even from dream to dream. By the time you are aware of a sign, the next moment you are awake.  Otherwise, you are just dreaming.

9.   Either you are dreaming or you are not dreaming.  Either you are sleeping or you are awake.

10.   The notion of signs of progress towards awakening is not valid and not helpful to the aspirant.

11.   A thousand different experiences may happen during your years of spiritual practice.

12.   Whatever sign there may be that the ego is about to come to its final end may only be known to you the moment before the ego comes to its final end.

13.   Thus being concerned with signs of progress during your years of practice is not helpful or valid.

14.   Progress may be imperceptible to the practitioner.

15.   A turbulent state can be a sign of progress if you are in the stage of doing battle with the ego.

16.   A peaceful state can be a sign of progress.

17.   The most helpful view for the aspirant is to not be concerned with signs of progress.

18.   If a list were given that was supposed to describe signs of progress, those who were not experiencing those signs would be discouraged.  Such a list would be false.  The human dream is a delusion.  Looking for signs of progress in a delusion is an error.

19.   Almost all experiences during spiritual practice are illusions.  Thus to look towards illusions for signs of progress towards awakening is folly.  This is true regardless of whether those illusions are blissful or sad.

20.    When a list of signs of progress is not given, what the aspirant has to fall back on is:  What was it that gave the aspirant the confidence that the method they are practicing is the most rapid and direct means to eternal bliss?

21.    In the case of the Awareness Watching Awareness Method, it is the fact that one's attention is focused exclusively on the background of awareness that makes it the most direct and rapid means.  In other words, your true Self is awareness.  The most rapid and direct means to the direct perception of your awareness is your awareness.  That makes it the most direct practice with no distractions or detours.

22.    Your first year of practice might be mostly turbulence.  Your second year of practice might be mostly peaceful or blissful.

23.    Or your first year of practice might be mostly peaceful or blissful and your second year of practice might be mostly turbulent.

24.    At some point the ego tries to stop the practice or progress of most people.  The ego can do this at almost any time, even after someone has been practicing for years.  That is one reason why half of this book has been devoted to exposing the ego, the ego's tricks, and how to reduce and finally end those tricks.

25.    Some people tend to not pay much attention to chapter's one through five and go directly to the Awareness Watching Awareness practice.  That is okay.  However, when the ego puts an end to the practice or makes the practice miserable, then it may be time to go back to the beginning with chapters one through five, with an emphasis on chapter five.

## EXPERIENCES

26.    There are trillions of possibilities regarding what you might experience while engaged in spiritual practice.

27.    Almost everything you experience during your spiritual practice should be ignored.    Some notable exceptions are if you have symptoms of a heart attack such as chest pains, etc. you should stop practicing and immediately call an ambulance.  If your smoke detector sounds its alarm, you should stop practicing and make sure there is no fire in your house.

28.    With the exceptions of those events which are an emergency or extremely urgent, almost everything else in the environment, body and inner experience should be ignored during your practice sessions.

29.    The goal is to perceive the seer.

30.    Almost any experience you have, including those you consider to be spiritual experiences, are the seen and not the seer.   They are the perceived, not the perceiver.  Therefore, they should be ignored.

31.    Experiences can be created from the power of suggestion.

32.    Two different spiritual groups, who as part of a spiritual teaching are taught that they can expect two different kinds of spiritual experiences, will tend to have experiences that match what they have been told to expect, even if they are practicing the same method. This is an example of the power of suggestion.  This is also an example of the power of illusion.

33.   It should not be a surprise to you that the mind can create an experience from the power of suggestion since it is now presenting the illusion to you that there is a planet called earth where there is in fact no such planet.  This same principle applies to the universe, etc

34.   Give people a list of the signs of spiritual progress and the mind can create such experiences. Unless the ego wants them to move onto a different practice or path in which case the ego may be unwilling to produce such experiences.

35.   Tell people what sort of experiences they can expect from a practice and the mind can create such experiences.  Unless the ego wants them to move onto a different practice or path in which case the ego may be unwilling to produce such experiences.

36.   Almost all experiences are distractions and detours.  A few of the most dangerous types will be listed here.  Now the question is how to list a few such possible experiences without the power of suggestion? The answer to that is: you keep in mind that it is just as likely that you will never have any of the experiences listed below during your spiritual practice as that you will have some of them.  As long as you keep in mind that these are only some of the possibilities, and that it is possible that you will never experience any of them, then the power of suggestion can be reduced or eliminated.

37.   It is possible during your spiritual practice to experience an entity that you communicate with. While you are sitting with your eyes closed you may see that entity in your mind's eye or you may hear it. If you see it, the list of possible forms it could have are almost endless.  It can have any color, shape or form.

148

38.  It may be an entity you are entirely unfamiliar with.

39.  Or it may be an entity that you are familiar with such as a Buddhist might think he is communicating with Buddha or a Christian might think he is communicating with Christ.  With a Hindu there are thousands of possibilities such as Siva or Krsna.

40.  Keep in mind it may be that you never experience any entity of any kind during your spiritual practice.  What is written here is for those people who do have such an experience during their practice.

41.  If you do experience any entity during your practice the best thing is to ignore the entity and do not communicate with it.  The reason for this is that an entity, even if the entity appears to be kind, is usually never what it appears to be.  Just as people can misrepresent themselves in the world and appear kind at first and later you discover they are not really kind and do not really have your best interest at heart; the same applies to entities you experience in spiritual practice or in meditation or contemplation.

42.  Whatever you experience during spiritual practice, ignore it and turn your attention away from it and towards the background of awareness.  Turn your attention away from the seen and towards the seer.  Turn your attention away from the known and towards the knower.  Turn your attention away from the heard and towards the hearer.

43.  You may experience a place, a realm, or another dimension.  The place may have entities in it.  It may seem to be the most wonderful, loving, beautiful place you have ever seen.  Ignore it.

44. All realms, all places, all dimensions are temporary illusions. The Reality is not a place and has no places in it. Thus even if you manage to live what seems like a trillion earth years in what seems to be a beautiful wonderful realm or place, it will come to an end. Then you will be right back in the cycle of births and deaths. For example: one hundred million imaginary lifetimes of suffering in realms that are not pleasant.

45. There may be entities in the beautiful realms that try and convince you that those realms are eternal. Don't believe those entities. No place is eternal. No realm is eternal. All realms and all places had a beginning in time and will have an end in time.

46. There are entities that initiate what seems like a fascinating relationship. They convince you to let them take you to another realm and then you will be placed in a prison. Your protection is to ignore all entities, even those entities that seem very benevolent to you. If you do meet an entity it is unlikely that it will be the type of entity that takes prisoners. Therefore, this is not something to worry about. The key point is to ignore all entities whether they seem kind or not.

47. Keep in mind that you may never experience any realm or place or entity. This is written for those who do experience a realm or place or entity.

48. That which is temporary is not the goal. That which is temporary will not free you from sorrow.

49. With any temporary experience, including a very blissful experience, you will end up right back where you started from – with suffering.

50. Temporary happiness, temporary bliss, temporary love, or temporary peace will not free you.

51. A temporary experience will not free you.

52. A temporary entity or place may seem to help, however; in the end they will not have produced any real help. They produce harm at least as a detour.

53. Almost anything you experience during spiritual practice is a distraction, a detour. It is best to ignore all that you experience during spiritual practice by turning your attention away from the experience and towards the experiencer.

## THE FINAL GOAL

54. What is the goal of practice? It is to bring the ego and its suffering and illusions to a final end so that only the true Self whose nature is Infinite-Eternal-Awareness-Love-Bliss remains.

55. What is most important is already described in #54 above. An attempt will be made to describe the final goal further; however, such descriptions are not what is most important. The fact that when the imposter self ends, all suffering ends for all eternity and that the True Self has never had any suffering in all eternity and is always absolutely perfect love-bliss is what is most important.

56. Suppose you try to describe the taste of pineapple juice to someone who has never tasted it. You say it is both sweet and tart at the same time. There are many juices that are both sweet and tart and none of them taste like pineapple juice. Thus you have failed to convey the taste through words.

57. If one cannot convey the taste of pineapple juice through words, how can the final Reality be described through words since the final Reality is not within the human frame of reference?

58. Describing the final Reality as Infinite-Eternal-Awareness-Love-Bliss is the closest one can come in words without straying too far from the human frame of reference.

59. In the final Reality, which is the only Reality, there are no worlds, no places, no dimensions, no universe, no realms, no forms, no time, no things, no beings and almost nothing that any word in the dictionary points towards.

60. In the final Reality, which is the only Reality, there are no humans, no animals, no planets, no stars, and no earth.

61. The final Reality is infinite awareness aware of infinite awareness. The final Reality, which is the only Reality, is infinite awareness aware of itself and itself is infinite awareness.

62. In all of eternity the final Reality has never been aware of anything other than infinite awareness-love-bliss. Awareness-love-bliss are not three, it is one.

63. In all of eternity the final Reality, which is the true Self, has never been aware of a human, or a world or suffering of any kind.

64. Humans, animals, earth, planets, stars, other realms, entities, places, time, dimensions, and that which almost every word in the dictionary points towards is part of the ego dream.

65.   When the ego comes to its final end, the dream ends and almost everything that the words in the dictionary point towards disappears.

66.   When the ego comes to its final end, what remains is Infinite-Eternal-Awareness-Love-Bliss and nothing ever reappears.  The planets, the stars, and almost everything that the words in the dictionary point towards never reappear.  They were all part of the dream.  Upon awakening, the dream disappears.

67.   The state humans consider to be their real life, the state that occurs when they wake up from sleep is a type of dream.  You could call it the waking-dream. The type of dream that occurs when humans are sleeping could be called the sleeping-dream.

68.   There are many differences between the waking-dream and the sleeping-dream.  For example there is a sense of continuity in the waking-dream.   Humans wake up into the story where the story left off.

69.   When the ego comes to its final end, both the waking-dream and the sleeping-dream end.

70.   When the ego comes to its final end, there is no longer the perception of a body or a world.

71.   Suppose you have a friend named Joe.  Suppose that Joe is one of those rare one in a million humans who succeeds in ending the ego illusion.  From the moment of the ending of the ego illusion Joe no longer has any perception of a body or a world. Yet from your perspective, assuming you are one who is still dreaming the human dream, you will still perceive Joe's body functioning normally.  You will see Joe walking, talking, eating and going about daily activities.

72.  An example to make this clearer is sleepwalking. Sleepwalkers may get up from the bed, go to the refrigerator, grab a glass of milk, and drink the glass of milk all while remaining asleep. The state of the one who has ended the ego is not identical with sleepwalking; this example is provided because the human mind tends to start with the assumption that the sages body only being perceptible to a third party onlooker is something incomprehensible.

73.  Here is yet another example. There are two friends named Sally and Joe. Joe is an astronaut. Joe takes a ship to the moon. Sally goes to sleep at night and has a dream. In the dream she is talking to Joe. But Joe is really on the moon. Therefore, even though Sally sees Joe walking and talking and sees Joe still living on the earth in her dream, Joe is not really on the earth. This also is just an example to attempt to make something more comprehensible that humans find difficult to comprehend. The awakened sage has not gone to some other place. In the case of an awakened sage the dream has ended that contained the place. Both the sleeping-dream and the waking-dream have ended for the awakened sage.

74.  Often when a human wakes up from a sleeping-dream, they have no memory of the sleeping-dream. Or they have a memory only for a minute or so upon awakening and then they cannot remember their sleeping-dream. The sage who has awakened from both the sleeping-dream and the waking-dream has no memory of ever having been human. Yet to one who is still dreaming it will appear that the sage is still carrying on normal physical life. The one still dreaming creates a waking-dream that includes the appearance of the body of the awakened sage.

75.  When you go to sleep at night and have a sleeping-dream all that appears in your sleeping-dream is just your own consciousness.  All the people you communicate with and all the places are really just your own consciousness.  They are not real.  They are your consciousness appearing as people, places, events and things.  Therefore what they really are is just one consciousness that has the ability to appear as everything in the dream.

76.  The example given in #75 above applies to the waking-dream also.  Everything you perceive in the waking-dream, which is what humans call real life, is one consciousness that has the ability to appear as the earth, people, animals, plants, stars, etc.  In other words one consciousness that has the ability to appear as everything including almost everything that the words in the dictionary point towards.  That one consciousness appears as both things and actions.

77.  There is a description that is even closer to the truth of the final Reality.  That is that the final Reality never appears as the earth, humans or almost anything that the words in the dictionary point towards.  The final Reality always remains as it is and there has never been a human, planet or almost anything the words in the dictionary point towards in the final Reality.

78.  One can use the example of a movie theatre.  In some places this may be called cinema.  The light inside the light bulb in the projector represents the final Reality or in other words the True Self.  The film represents thoughts, feelings, emotions, the body, the five senses, etc.  On the screen a world is seen.  However, inside the light which is inside the light bulb inside the projector there is no world, no movie, no people etc.

79.   All of what is described here can be known in direct experience by bringing the ego to its final end.

80.   The difference between the deep dreamless sleep state and the final Reality is that in the deep dreamless sleep state there appears to be unconsciousness.   In the final Reality there is awareness that never changes and is always aware.

81.   When you wake up from a sleeping-dream, where did the world and people you dreamed about go?   They did not go anywhere.   They were never really there even while you were dreaming.   So it is when you wake up from the human waking-dream. The planets, people, animals, plants, stars, etc. were never really there.   They seemed real while you were dreaming them in the waking-dream, just like what you experience in the sleeping-dream seems real while you are dreaming it.   When you wake up from the waking-dream, which happens when the ego comes to its final end, the planets, people, animals, plants, stars, etc. disappear, similar to how whatever you dream in the sleeping-dream disappears upon your waking up.

82.   Imagine an ocean of consciousness.   Instead of an ocean of water, this is an ocean of consciousness. Almost all of the waves on this ocean of consciousness have developed the habit of never looking down.   They only look out horizontally.   Because they only look out horizontally all they see are what appears to be billions of separate waves.   They assume that there is no ocean, only separate waves.   One day one of these waves has the courage to dive deep down within itself and discovers the ocean.   This wave discovers that there is no line that separates it from the ocean.   This wave discovers that there are no waves, there is only the ocean.

83.   Wave is a concept created by imagining there is a bottom line that separates the wave from the ocean. There are no waves, there is only the ocean. This can be known in direct experience.

## SPIRITUAL PRACTICE

84.   Because the true Self is eternally perfect awareness-love-bliss and eternally free of all suffering, some people think there is no need for spiritual practice.   Such a notion is an ego preservation strategy.   The purpose of practice is not to gain the true Self.   The purpose of practice is to remove the illusion of a body, a world, suffering, etc. so that what remains is only the eternal experience of the True Self.

85.   In other words, those who have let the ego trick them into thinking there is no need for spiritual practice, because the True Self is eternally free of suffering, etc., are still having the experience of suffering, a body, a world, etc.   Thus their experience is not consistent with their concept that the True Self is eternally free of suffering and perfectly blissful.   This is an example of intellectual "spirituality."   This is an example of people confusing a journey through concepts, ideas, beliefs and opinions with an authentic spiritual journey.   Practice leads to the direct experience of Infinite-Eternal-Awareness-Love-Bliss.

86.   A journey through spiritual concepts, ideas, beliefs, teachings and opinions is a journey through illusion.

87.   Practice is what is essential.   It must not be a spiritual practice that is created by the ego for the purpose of preserving the ego.

88.   With the Awareness Watching Awareness Method, the practice is the progress.   The habit has been developed of always looking outward towards the seen. The Awareness Watching Awareness Method reverses this.   Every time a thought arises, or the tendency to look outward, the attention is taken away from the thought and turned towards the seer.

89.   Thus with the Awareness Watching Awareness Method a new habit is developed and the practice is the progress.

90.   A question might arise why does the Awareness Watching Awareness Method focus attention on one's ordinary everyday background of awareness instead of attempting to look for Infinite Awareness?  Here is an example that can answer this question:  Imagine that you live in a mansion that has thousands of dark rooms and you are trying to find the sunlight.  If you focus your attention on a beam of sunlight that enters one of the rooms and follow that beam and trace its origin you can find the source of that light – the Sun.  However, if you hold the concept of the Sun and ignore the beam of sunlight that enters some of the rooms, you could open a thousand doors in dark rooms and never find the Sun.   In this example the Sun represents the Infinite Awareness which is the True Self.  The beam of sunlight   represents   your   ordinary   everyday consciousness.  If people hold some concept of infinite awareness and try to find it, they will never find it. Your own everyday background of awareness is the path to Infinite Awareness, as sunlight is to the Sun.

91.   Another example: Imagine a planet where all of the people were born and raised and spent their entire lives in a movie theatre.  Almost all of them believed the movie they were seeing on the screen was real.

Their attention was so fixed on the screen that they never bothered to turn their heads around 180 degrees to see the projector's light. One of them had the courage to turn his head around 180 degrees and he saw the projector's light. He did not know what it was, but he followed that light until he found the projector. He went back and told the people that what they were seeing on the screen was not real.

He told them that to find the projector they would have to turn their heads around 180 degrees. Due to the long habit of always keeping their attention fixed on the movie screen, fear of the unknown, their belief that the movie was real, and their disbelief in what he was telling them, very few bothered to turn their heads around 180 degrees to see the light from the projector. Some of those who did follow his instructions turned their heads immediately back to the screen. They were used to the illusion and afraid of the Truth. Others did not sustain their attempt to find the projector long enough to find it. After all it is difficult to find the projector in the dark. One has to pass through a number of doors to find it. Once in a while someone actually persevered long enough to find the projector.

92. If you are in a dark room, spiritual practice is like opening the drapes or curtains. If a person says the Sun is there, therefore there is no need to open the drapes, that person will always live in darkness. So it is with those who say there is no need for spiritual practice.

93. There was a spiritual teacher who for more than fifty years gave talks around the world. He said there is no need for practice. He said any movement of the me center (ego) helps to perpetuate the me center.

That might sound logical; however, what are the actual results? Towards the end of his life it was this teacher's view that none of the people who had attended his talks or read his books had succeeded in ending the me center. Practice is essential. Talking you out of spiritual practice is an ego preservation strategy. There is another way to understand the need for practice: Most of the people of the world are not doing any spiritual practice. They are also not being liberated from this no-practice. Thus it is essential to find a practice that is effective.

## THE LOVING CONSCIOUSNESS METHOD

94. This is a new method being introduced with this, the sixth edition of this book. This is a primary method meaning that it is to be practiced every day for as many hours per day as you can create by dropping all unnecessary activities. The preliminary instructions are the same as for the Awareness Watching Awareness Method and the definition of Awareness and Consciousness is the same also. See chapter seven for both.

## PRACTICE INSTRUCTIONS
## FOR THE LOVING CONSCIOUSNESS METHOD
### (95)

95. Shut your eyes. Love your consciousness. Continue to feel love towards your awareness throughout the practice session.

Worship your consciousness.
Cherish your consciousness.
Value your consciousness.

If the instructions to worship, cherish and value your consciousness do not convey any meaning that you can put into practice then you can ignore those instructions and just use the instructions to feel love towards your consciousness. Your awareness loving your awareness. What makes this simple practice unique is the way awareness and consciousness are defined in this book. In this practice you are not loving thoughts, feelings, etc. You are loving the background of awareness.

96.    The question may arise which of the three primary practices, the Awareness Watching Awareness Method, the Abandon Release Method or the Loving Consciousness Method should you practice?    Try practicing the Awareness Watching Awareness Method first.  Practice it for as long as the ego will allow you to practice it.   If the ego will allow you to practice it permanently then continue to practice the Awareness Watching Awareness Method.

97.    If the ego tries to stop you from practicing whatever method you are practicing, try to persevere. If the ego wins the battle and you stop practicing the Awareness Watching Awareness Method, then try practicing the Abandon Release Method.  If the ego stops you from practicing the Abandon Release Method, then try practicing the Loving Consciousness Method.

98.    Hopefully you can practice each method for at least one year before moving onto another method. That way you can gain some skill with the method.

99.    You can continue to practice the method you like best.   Or, if you tire of one method you could try alternating, practicing the Awareness Watching Awareness Method for one year, then switching to the Abandon Release Method for the second year, then for

the third year switching to the Loving Consciousness Method, then for the fourth year back to the Awareness Watching Awareness Method. All three methods are complimentary. In other words skill in one of the methods helps to develop skill in the other methods.

100. The question may arise who or what does the practice? It is the ego that leads one to practice. Usually the ego leads one to practice a method that will allow the ego to continue. Thus the human delusion and human evil continues. However, it is possible for the ego to see the need for its own end. Chapter five reveals many ways to show the ego the need for its own end. One of the most important of these is the exercise in chapter five verses 14, 15 and 16. That is the exercise to face the ocean of human suffering, sorrow, deceit, cruelty etc. Usually humans only face a few drops in that ocean. Usually humans block that ocean from their awareness. Thus the extent of human evil, or in other words the ego's evil, is not seen.

A human might be willing to look at part of one war. However it is very rare that a human is willing to look at what fifteen thousand wars in the last five thousand years really means. Seeing what happened to each and every individual human in those wars. In addition to the wars, trillions of acts of violence have occurred. Billions of lies are told by humans each and every day including today. Billions of acts of cruelty occur every day including today. Yet all this is still only a few drops in the ocean of human suffering and evil. This is a case where a picture is worth a thousand words. Photographs of human bodies after the acts of violence have occurred can convey much more than mere words. Billions of acts of verbal deceit, conning, and cheating occur every day including today. Humans lie not only to each other but to themselves every day.

101. There is a further step one can take to see the extent of the ego's vast network of deception, cruelty, insincerity, etc. That is to see how usually what humans call good is also the ego's evil in a hidden form.

102. The capacity of thought is tremendous. All of the information in all of the books that have ever been printed has been created by thought. All of the information on the entire World Wide Web has been created by thought. All the technology from going to the moon to computers, etc. has been created by thought. Even in one single human the possible combinations that thought, ideas, concepts, etc. can take number in the trillions. If human thought were basically something sincere with good pure motives, life would be quite different. However, thought is not something basically sincere with good pure motives. Thought is something insincere and deceptive with sinister motives. Thought has trillions of layers of self deception. When something that is basically deceptive and dishonest has such a vast network of thought to work with, it is not difficult to see how thought has been able to keep almost all humans prisoner for all of human history. Seeing the extent of the self-deception, thought's layer upon layer of self-deception, dishonesty, insincerity and thought's ability to hide what it is doing from its imaginary self, is the key to understanding the ancient human trap. It is also the key to understanding how all of the religious and spiritual teachings of the past serve the ego.

103. Thought hides its true nature. Thought blocks out its sinister, deceptive nature and pretends to itself that it is sincere and good. That which has produced 15,000 wars in the last 5,000 years and trillions of lies is not sincere and good.

104. Self honesty begins by beginning to face the insincerity, deceptiveness, evil and cruelty of thought.

105. Progress in self honesty is seeing that the extent of thought's insincerity, deceptiveness, evil and cruelty is much vaster than one ever suspected. Something like going through one's life thinking that a lake of insincerity, deceptiveness, evil and cruelty was the extent of it and discovering that the network of thought was not a lake but an ocean of insincerity, deceptiveness, evil and cruelty. It is important to see this ocean both in other humans and in one's own mind also. See the vast network of thought.

106. If one does a good job of seeing what is pointed out in 100 through 105 above, then statements such as "All the spiritual teachings of the past serve the ego" will not seem like too strong a statement. The ego has not left the spiritual teachings of the past untouched. The ego has made sure that they serve it. If you face the ocean of human evil and suffering, including the fifteen thousand wars in the last five thousand years, you can see that humans are delusional. The spiritual and religious teachings of the past are a product of that same delusion.

107. It is not only religious or spiritual thought that serves the ego. Almost all human thought serves the ego. By looking at the results, i.e. the history of human evil, one can see that is true. It is not one little isolated event of cruelty, deception, insincerity etc., it is trillions of acts of cruelty, deception, insincerity, etc.

108. One reason why it is so important to become aware of the ocean of human suffering, deception, insincerity, cruelty, etc. is because that is one of the steps towards ending it.

The very fact that humans pretend that human insincerity is not omnipresent is one of the factors that has always allowed human insincerity to flourish. Making excuses and creating explanations, rationalizations, and justifications for human evil has been one of the primary factors that has allowed human evil to continue. If one denies all those excuses, explanations, rationalizations and justifications and instead just see human evil as evil that is a first step towards the ending of human evil. If you do not like the word evil you can use the words cruelty, deception, hurtfulness, harmfulness, lying, cheating, conning, violence (both physical and verbal), insincerity, dishonesty, pretense, apathy, hatred.

109. Suppose there is a man who considers himself to be very logical, rational and scientifically minded. This man rejects all the religious and spiritual teachings. He thinks he is a body and when the body dies that is the end of it. Therefore, whatever pleasure he can get out of this brief material life is in his view the purpose of his life. The spiritual teachings of the past have stated that there is more to what a human is than just his body-mind. They have stated that the true nature of the human is eternal. It is understandable that the man has rejected those spiritual teachings that rely on belief to establish this, and that state that one will find the truth of this when the body dies, because those teachings are a distortion of the original teachings of the founders of those religions, and are changes made to those teachings for religious-political or religious-business reasons. However, there are also the experiential spiritual teachings that are not relying on beliefs. They say do such and such a practice and you can experience the results. Now this man has a choice. He is offered the possibility of eternal perfect love-bliss or a temporary brief life and death.

If this man were truly rational, logical, sane, etc. the potential gain is so great he would make the decision to do a spiritual practice that can reveal to him his true Self and thus live eternally in love-bliss free of all suffering. However, he holds the belief that there is no such eternal true Self. He does not know there is no eternal true Self. He just believes there is no eternal true Self. He is not rational, logical or sane, although he believes he is rational, logical and sane.

What is it that leads him to the decision not to do a spiritual practice that has the potential to reveal to him his true Self and let him enter the ocean of eternal bliss? It is the ego. The pro-religious believer, and the anti-religious disbeliever who thinks he is so rational, are both lost in belief. Belief is not Truth.

110. If somehow the ego allows either the one who believes or the one who disbelieves in the true eternal nature of the human to see the great value in becoming a knower, which is of course not a believer or a disbeliever, then there are a huge number of practices that they could try.

111. There are Hindu, Buddhist, Christian Mysticism, and Sufi practices. There are practices that do not fall within such popular categories. Explaining in detail why all such practices do not lead to the ego's final end and how all such teachings and practices serve the ego would require a large book. Maybe one of the future volumes in this series will do just that. However, when one names specific teachings and begins to list the defects in those teachings and how they serve the ego, many people tend to have a strong emotional reaction because of their attachment to and investment in such beliefs. Thus it is more helpful to point out the quotes from those traditions that do not serve the ego.

Also, even if one points out the defects etc., if the desire for Truth and Freedom is not there they will not see what is being pointed out.

112. If the desire for Truth and Freedom is great enough the aspirant can see how the spiritual teachings of the past serve the ego without it being pointed out to them. Ask the question: How does this spiritual teaching serve the ego? Then examine the spiritual teaching to find the answer to that question.

113. Different spiritual teachings have different goals. The ego likes a goal that is at least somewhat familiar to it. In one of the world's religions the goal was to end the ego and suffering and the original teachings said the world appearance and the cycle of births and deaths would end also. Later that religion split into groups of very different teachings and in those teachings they said in the final goal the world returns. It is very easy to see the ego contamination. The ego wants its world. So the ego changed the goal into one in which the world returns. The original teacher of that religion gave a lot of talks and thousands of pages of teachings resulted. However, those teachings were not recorded until hundreds of years after his death. Thus the teachings cannot be relied upon as an accurate representation of what he actually said. He is very wordy and never seems to get to any essential points in his talks. His teachings are very complicated.

114. More than one of the world's religions worships an entity that they consider to be the Supreme Being. According to their scriptures this Supreme Being drowned his children (almost all of humanity) in a flood that he (the entity they consider to be the Supreme Being) deliberately created. In their scriptures this same entity admits to creating evil.

Many other evil acts perpetrated by this entity are recorded in their scriptures. The goal of these religions is to spend eternity with this entity. Why would anyone wish to spend eternity with an entity who is a mass murderer who using the maximum of its extremely limited intelligence can find no better solution to the problem of its children's misbehavior than to murder them in a deliberately created flood?

Part of the answer to this question is in how religious ideas are spread. Usually people are taught beliefs of a particular religion from childhood. Read books about Memes or Memetics to learn more about how religious and other beliefs are spread from human to human much like a virus. Thus the beliefs of a particular religion become a basic part of the persons mind. There is usually a lifetime bias towards the religion the person was taught. Sometimes the religion contains terrible threats of eternal punishment. Thus the person can no longer think clearly about the fact that the goal of the religion is to spend eternity with a stupid, evil mass murderer. Incidentally the humans that followed the flood were just as evil as those that preceded it and thus the stupid evil entity's solution failed. All those people murdered for nothing. Human thought can always find an explanation or justification for evil. For example thought might say that the flood was not literal but symbolic. However, if that were the case that story could have stated that it was only symbolic. The fact that it did not state that it was symbolic of something else but presented it as a real flood created by the entity they consider to be the Supreme Being, an entity that announces that the purpose of the flood is to kill almost all of the animals and humans on earth because they are evil, reveals one of the defects in the teaching.

If every time thought tries to explain evil away you do not believe the explanation but instead just say no to the evil, then everything will start to change for you. You would then walk away from such a religion or spiritual teaching and never return. One might wonder how such a religion gets converts. The answer is that those trying to convert you do not say "How would you like to spend eternity with an entity who using the maximum of its extremely limited intelligence thought the best solution for its misbehaving children, who were almost all the humans living at the time, was to murder them in a deliberately created flood?" No they don't say that, instead they talk about eternal life, etc.

115. Yet another of the world's religions has many different teachers and many different teachings. One of the most popular in this religion is an entity they consider to be the Supreme Being incarnated on earth. There is a battlefield. There are two opposing armies. The leader of one of the armies tells this entity that he does not want to fight. He has so many relatives in the opposing army. The entity, using the maximum of its extremely limited intelligence, tells the leader to go ahead and fight.

If humans find themselves in a battlefield situation and they do not fight, then they may be killed. It is understandable why humans usually choose to fight in such a situation. However, when an entity that is supposed to be the Supreme Being can find no better solution than for people to murder each other, then you can be assured there is something seriously wrong with that entity, that the entity is not the Supreme Being and that there is something quite evil in that teaching. Thought can create an explanation or justification for anything no matter how evil it is.

For example thought can say it was not a real battlefield. The armies represented psychological states that needed to be battled. If that is the case the story could have made that clear. The fact that the story did not include such an explanation is the evidence of one of the defects in the teaching. If every time thought tries to justify evil, you do not believe in thought's explanation or justification, then you will begin to see what you have never seen before. It will then be much easier to avoid evil or defective spiritual teachings. You would then walk away from such a religious or spiritual teaching and never return.

116. Suppose you go to sleep tonight and have a dream. In that dream one thousand scientists present ten thousand pages of evidence to support a certain conclusion. Maybe for example the conclusion that everything experienced in meditation including the most profound experiences are created by the brain. When you wake up from the dream you find that the scientists and all their evidence were just a dream and their evidence and conclusions you now know had no validity. While dreaming the dream seems real.

117. Science can be very helpful to navigate the waking-dream and make the waking-dream less painful. If your body has symptoms of illness, go to see a modern medical doctor.

118. Where science fails is in being helpful with waking up from the waking-dream. The ego in the scientist is just as dedicated to continuing the waking-dream as is the ego in the religious believer, the philosopher and almost all other human beings.

119. There are current scientific discoveries that support the notion that all is one consciousness.

120. However, science is constantly changing. In the year three thousand, the views of science of the year two thousand will be thought to be absurd. In the year four thousand the views of science of the year three thousand will be thought to be absurd. Science is for the purpose of discovering that which is relatively truer. Science is not for the purpose of experiencing the Absolute Truth that has never changed in all eternity and that will never change in all eternity.

121. The ego only pretends to want freedom, except in very rare cases. Therefore, the religious person is not seeking Freedom and the experience of the Infinite-Awareness. The religious person is only pretending to themselves that they want eternal Freedom-Bliss-Love. The scientist is only pretending to want Truth. Almost all humans serve the false ego.

122. Suppose someone begins the study and practice of a spiritual or religious teaching. Thought says "I am sincere; I really intend to attain the goal of this teaching." However, there is another deeper layer of thought that knows it really has no intention of ever attaining the goal of the spiritual teaching. Thus the aspirants imagine they are sincere when in fact they are not sincere. This is an example of self-deception. Self-honesty is the cure. Self-honesty begins by actually becoming aware of the layers upon layers of self-deception. Devote your life to Truth and Freedom.

123. It is not all gloomy and bleak. There is something wonderful and extremely beautiful. You can wake up and live eternally in Infinite-Awareness-Love-Bliss, free of all suffering. Your true Self is that now. Wishing you success in bringing the imposter (ego) to its final end. Start the day with love.
Fill the day with love. End the day with love.

If it seems that a discovery is so unique that no else has discovered it, then usually humans will discount such a discovery as not being valid. Although the particular combination of teachings in this book is found only here, many of the separate discoveries can be found in other teachings. For those of you who think that a discovery can only be valid when the same discovery has been made at different times by what appears to be different teachers, on this page are listed sources where supporting quotes can be read.

You can start by visiting www.seeseer.com

Vernon Howard was the master at exposing the tricks of the ego and human insincerity including the insincerity of spiritual students. The recordings of his classes do a much better job of this than his books. For information about where you can order recordings of his classes you can visit www.anewlife.org

To learn more about how ideas and beliefs are spread from human to human like a virus and are looking out for their own interests and do not have their hosts best interests at heart, read books about Memes and Memetics. You will find a list of books at seeseer.com

The Awareness Watching Awareness Method was described by Sri Ramana Maharshi in the book *The Garland of Guru's Sayings, Guru Vachaka Kovai* translated by Prof. K. Swaminathan. Go to seeseer.com for more information. Ramana Maharshi also gave many warnings against intellectualism in that and other books.

Information about where to find Christian Mysticism, Buddhist and Sufi quotes that support the teachings in this book can be found at seeseer.com

Printed in the United States
121029LV00003B/352-357/P